GOD HAS A WAY

*Trusting That God Is Caring for You
Even When It Doesn't Feel Like It*

Howard C. Earle, Jr.

Copyright © 2022 by **Howard C. Earle, Jr.**

All rights reserved. No part of this publication may be reproduced, distributed, or transmitted in any form or by any means, without prior written permission.

Unless otherwise noted, all Scripture quotations are taken from the Holy Bible, New International Version®, NIV® Copyright © 1973, 1978, 1984, 2011 by Biblica, Inc.® Used by permission. All rights reserved worldwide.

Scripture quotations marked (NKJV) are taken from the New King James Version®. Copyright © 1982 by Thomas Nelson, Inc. Used by permission. All rights reserved.

Renown Publishing
www.renownpublishing.com

God Has a Way / Howard C. Earle, Jr.
ISBN-13: 978-1-952602-97-9

Praise for God Has a Way **by Howard C. Earle, Jr.**

A biblically based volume of how God acts in the places we least expect. This book will bless you and set you free!
Kraig L. Pullam
Pastor of Shiloh Fort Worth

God Has a Way is encouraging and soft-spoken in revealing God's steady and ever-present hand in the lives of His children. Pastor Earle's writing yields a voice of humility as he reflects on the awesome nature of our God's unceasing providence, despite our human stumbles and flaws. I will keep this work close by for those moments when I and those near to me need companionship and reassurance in our loneliest of times.
Jeff Huegli
President and CEO of Beacon Hill at Eastgate

Awesomely inspiring! *God Has a Way* hit the mark regarding my own questions about failure, challenges, and correction in my life and others'. Dr. Earle shines the light on the heart of God, His sovereign will toward His children, and the unique bond of love that motivates His judgment and compassion for the saved, the sinner, and the lost. This work is the answer to the question, "Does God care?"
Rev. Dr. Andre J. Lewis
Pastor of New Faith Church, Houston, Texas

In this book, God has used Dr. Earle's lived experiences to show that He has the answer to life's frustrations, difficulties, and setbacks. Dr. Earle writes, as a credible witness, that God certainly always has a way, and His way leads to life ... more abundantly. Buy this book and be enlightened and encouraged, regardless of what happens in this life.

Dr. Addis Moore
Sr. Pastor of Mt. Zion Baptist Church, Kalamazoo, Michigan

To Mom and Dad, for laying a foundation upon which my tower of faith and understanding continue to be erected.

And to my wife, K'Sandra, and our amazing children—Zachary, Dylan Camille, and Natalie. Thank you for being the wind beneath my wings and allowing me to soar. Let's go with God and see what He is up to!

CONTENTS

Foreword by Darryl P. Plunkett iii

His Ways Are Not Our Ways vii

Holy GPS 1

Setbacks, Setups, and Comebacks 19

It's Not What It Looks Like 33

The Ministry of Delay 47

Storms as Classrooms 61

Finding Peace in the Pieces 73

Trust God's Eye 85

Grace Over Stones 99

The Truth About Failure 113

How God Makes Good 125

About the Author 137

About Renown Publishing 139

Notes 141

FOREWORD

Foreword by Darryl P. Plunkett

God Has a Way is a should-read book for anyone who professes to be a Christian. It is a must-read for those who do not know the truth of God. This book reminds the former group, and informs the latter group, that it is more than beneficial to know and believe that *Trusting That God Is Caring for You Even When It Doesn't Feel Like It.* Trusting Him makes a world of difference in how we live this life's journey. As a deacon under the pastorate of Rev. Dr. Howard C. Earle, Jr., I have benefited tremendously from his preaching and teaching for the last thirteen years, including the sermons in this book.

God Has a Way: Trusting That God Is Caring for You Even When It Doesn't Feel Like It is a compilation of ten sermons that discern and describe how God works in our lives for His glory and our gain. While all the homilies in this book speak truth to power concerning how God cares for us, some contain messages from Pastor Earle, under the tutelage of the

Holy Spirit, that are specific to each individual's situation. For example, in Chapter Three, he speaks about how "It's Not What It Looks Like" and tells us that God knows our future in full detail. That's good news. And thank God that we do not, because I suspect many of us would avoid the valleys and tribulations in life just to get to the blessings. Fortunately, that is not how God works in our lives; otherwise, we may very well forget (or perhaps even worse, not know) what James wrote when he encouraged us to "consider it pure joy, my brothers and sisters, whenever you face trials of many kinds" (James 1:2).

Moreover, in Chapter Six, "Finding Peace in the Pieces" explains how God cares for us so much, He can and will take the broken pieces of our lives and help us to find the peace that "surpasses all understanding" (Philippians 4:7 NKJV). Pastor Earle tells us that being human is being broken, and it is not necessarily because we are bad people. Oftentimes, it is the sovereign will of God to show us how broken we are so we know that only He can put us together again.

During many of Pastor Earle's calls to discipleship after his sermons, I have heard him tell the congregants that "we cannot wait to accept Jesus Christ once we get ourselves together." The Scriptures say it differently, but just as powerfully: "without Me you can do nothing," God tells us, "but with Me all things are possible." Thanks be to God!

During some of our discussions, I came to know that Pastor Earle was hesitant to write this book. Nonetheless, he prayed and persevered to share with all who would be willing to read what the Holy Spirit has taught him. I commend him for this, because I know that it was not an easy task; however, I believed he could do it and told him so.

There are many ministers, pastors, and servants of God who have written theological books, can write theological books, or may write theological books. But this particular book project was assigned to Pastor Earle by the Holy Spirit, just as other books, sermons, and services are assigned to other men and women of God. Why? Certainly not because Pastor Earle is the only person capable of writing such a book, but because of the sovereign will of God to share what He has put on Pastor Earle's mind, heart, and spirit. God also gave him the ability and capacity to carry out His will. I look forward to reading Pastor Earle's next book and hope you do also.

To be clear, this is not a reference book. Instead, it is a volume that I believe should be read, in its entirety, by everyone. Though a person may read a specific chapter that is especially appropriate for what he or she is facing at present, all ten chapters can profit every reader—to be reminded that whatever the situation or circumstance, *God Has A Way*. He has a way for you, and He has a way for me. I strongly encourage you to read this book, because I don't want you to miss the impact *Trusting That God Is Caring for You Even When It Doesn't Feel Like It* will have on your life!

Darryl P. Plunkett, Ph.D.
Grand Rapids, Michigan

INTRODUCTION

His Ways Are Not Our Ways

"'For my thoughts are not your thoughts, neither are your ways my ways,' declares the LORD" (Isaiah 55:8). At face value, that seems like a conceited thing to say. It's especially a conceited statement for a God of love and grace to make to His beloved children. It's as if God is saying, "I don't have to answer to you. I can move on My own terms, and I don't have to abide by your rules."

But actually, God can say that. These statements are merely a sample of what makes God so uniquely different from and superior to us. To be totally transcendent, sufficient, all-knowing, ever-present, and all of the other attributes ascribed to Him makes Him like no other.

It is out of the "like no other" nature of God that we experience His care for us. The very title of this book sheds light on the truth that *God has a way* of caring for us. Furthermore, God has His own particular way of caring for us. He is not bound by time and space, and He operates according to His own logic and reason. Without those boundaries, the possibilities are infinite. It is out of this infinite well of resources and power that God cares for us.

Though a single book can only scratch the surface of how God cares for us in the most unusual-seeming ways, the following chapters embark on an unapologetic, biblically based exploration of how God chooses to act. We'll look at this topic through the lens of common experiences, such as failure, hardship, fulfillment, and other ups and downs of life's journey.

Sometimes, as we'll see, God chooses the long way instead of the shortest route. Other times, He allows us to suffer instead of delivering us. It seems insensitive to delay on purpose so that circumstances grow more urgent before He acts, yet God does this and other perplexing things. On the surface, it would seem that He is callous, aloof, and arrogant.

But such a characterization could not be less accurate. God has a way of allowing life to fall apart so that He can show us who really holds things together. He refuses to acquiesce to any cultural norms or pressures, and He goes to great lengths to make it clear and obvious that He is in total control.

It is my prayer that these pages would inspire, educate, encourage, and embolden you to trust God if you don't already know Him or trust Him more fully if you do have a relationship with Him. I encourage you to place yourself within the scriptural narratives recounted in these pages, allowing yourself to connect with the Israelites' uncertainty in the desert, the disciples' anxiety, Joseph's setbacks, Peter's failure, Paul's shipwreck, and the shame of the woman caught in adultery.

In these places of dissonance and tension, we can experience the length, breadth, and depth of God's love. He will defy the laws of nature, break the rules, beat the odds, and disregard the facts just to ensure that we reach our fullest potential. No matter the circumstances, we can rest in this fact: God has a way!

CHAPTER ONE

Holy GPS

> *When Pharaoh let the people go, God did not lead them on the road through the Philistine country, though that was shorter. For God said, "If they face war, they might change their minds and return to Egypt." So God led the people around by the desert road toward the Red Sea. The Israelites went up out of Egypt ready for battle.*
> —*Exodus 13:17–18*

In the 1960s, the U. S. Navy started conducting satellite navigation experiments. Then, in the 1970s, the Department of Defense launched its first navigation system, which became fully operational in 1993. This sophisticated system has now become widespread and transformative, changing how we live in our world. We know it as the Global Positioning System, or GPS.[1]

Have you wondered what life now would be like without GPS? How would your life be impacted? These days, it's simple for us to reach a destination knowing only the address. We rarely have to ask for directions, instead just saying, "Give me the address. My GPS will find it."

Are you old enough to recall giving directions prior to GPS? Often people would lead you by landmarks rather than by road or street names, giving only a rough idea of distances: "You have to go to the third or fourth street—you'll know it when you see the white house on the corner. Then keep going straight. If you see a brown house with a car on bricks in front, you've gone too far."

GPS is more sophisticated, giving you options for multiple routes and telling you in real time what's happening on any given route. A particular route might save you fifteen minutes if you're willing to pay tolls. Another way might be shorter in distance but delay you an hour because of an accident. It will point out stop signs, train tracks, and speed cameras. It will also help you find gas, rest stops, and restaurants when needed.

Of course, people in biblical times couldn't conceive of GPS technology. When the ancient Israelites were ready to travel to the land God had promised their ancestor Abraham, they could have relied on their own knowledge or on local guides. But most of all, they relied on their leader, Moses, and he relied on God.

After 430 years of slavery in Egypt, the nation of Israel reached a monumental turning point in her history. The Israelites had just passed through ten plagues, the last of which saw God's angel of death take the firstborn sons of Egypt (Exodus 12:29–30). As they left the land of their enslavement, perhaps the Israelites could still hear the wailing and weeping of their former masters. But the Israelite households had been spared because of the lamb's blood they smeared on their doorposts at God's command through Moses (Exodus 12:7). In fear, Pharaoh ordered the Israelites out of the land.

Over a million Israelites left Egypt and began the journey to the promised land of Canaan. In Exodus 13:17–18, the Bible says that God would lead them. He was selective in the way He would lead them, deciding on the longer route instead of the more direct route. Scripture tells us this was for a specific reason: God knew that the Israelites weren't ready for the kind of hardship they would face in Canaan. God was intentional about the means by which He delivered His people—through His servant Moses and the ten plagues—and also about the path they would take.

No one's circumstances stay the same throughout his or her life. We're all on our way toward a destiny, or destination. There is a Canaan, a promise and a specially planned experience, waiting for us all. There is a place where God wants you to be, other than the place you find yourself now, and He is meticulously moving you toward that new place.

We all aspire to something greater and grander for our lives, and if we could, we'd get there as soon as possible. But sometimes God programs a less direct route, a way that doesn't seem to be the fastest, into our GPS. As God led the nation of Israel, He has a way of leading us through life. He deliberately chooses our path, the terrain we'll cross, and the timing of our journey as He marches us from our point of departure to the place of our destiny, from one season of life to the next. God has an active role in our journey every step of the way.

We are all on our way somewhere, so we all need to understand certain truths about how God leads us where He wants us to go.

God Leads from a Heavenly Perspective

GPS tech has profoundly impacted life as we know it. The technology that was at one time used strictly for the military is now used by civilians. Companies like Amazon and Walmart use the technology to make deliveries. We now live in a time when we can shop, pick our items, purchase them, and receive them without ever leaving our homes.

Now, GPS doesn't function strictly from a ground-level view; it uses satellites positioned far beyond the earth's atmosphere. Signals bouncing off the satellites provide us with coordinates and help us see more clearly what's happening down on the ground, where we're located.

Similarly, God has a unique vantage point on your life because He is seated on His throne in heaven, from which He can see every possible route, every bump and pothole, every twist and crooked turn. He doesn't see the way we see, in chronological sequence and based on what's right in front of us. Instead, *God leads from a heavenly perspective*. He sees clearly around corners we can't. He knows in detail what will happen later today, tomorrow, next week, and next year, as if your whole life had already unfolded.

Because God sees all of life, we do ourselves a service when we yield to the route guidance He gives us. Though God very well might choose the long way, we can rest assured that it's the best way for us. The Apostle Paul said, "And we know that in all things God works for the good of those who love him, who have been called according to his purpose" (Romans 8:28). The long way and the short way, the mountain road and the valley road, the smooth path and the crooked path—God may lead you by any of these routes, but the way He leads you always works because He has a better vantage point than you do.

In your moments of frustration, know that God sees what you can't see. The route that seems unnecessarily long or difficult may be God's way of protecting or saving you. So declare your trust for Him as you undertake your journey through life.

God's choice of a certain route for each of us is an expression of His sovereign will. After all, He could have literally scooped the Israelites out of Egypt and dropped them in Canaan. He could have opened up a highway directly to the promised land. But He chooses the way He chooses for His reasons; that's His sovereign will.

The term *sovereign* is a foundational word for this entire book. As an adjective, the word means to possess supreme, unlimited, unqualified power or authority.[2] The United States of America is a sovereign nation, meaning that its government acts of its own accord, not requiring permission or approval from any other nation or power. Likewise, God needs no permission to act, and He acts from His own motivations.

Often, in difficult times, we want to cry out, "Why, God? Why?" *Why* is one of the toughest questions we wrestle with in this life. Why do good people die? Why do children die? Why do natural disasters and calamities claim so many lives? Why do our loved ones have to die from cancer? I don't try to answer those questions, but I can tell you these things: God knows why, He didn't make a mistake, and He had us in mind when He decided what would happen. That may be little consolation in the moment, but it's the truth.

Since we know this, we can surrender to His sovereign will, trusting Him to take care of us on our journey. As the hymn goes, "we'll understand it better by and by." [3]

If you're still not contented with this reasoning, consider that your rationality will never match the mind of God. Why? Because His thoughts are not our thoughts, and His ways are not our ways.

GOD HAS HIS OWN TIMING

Another fundamental truth about how God leads us is that *He operates in His own timing*. The road through Philistine country was shorter, but God chose the desert road by the Red Sea for Israel's journey because Israel reaching the promised land quickly was not His highest priority. If we knew our intended destination, we'd want to cut every corner and cut across every field to get there faster, bypassing every trouble and hardship. "If it's my land of promise," we'd reason, "why wait? Take me there right now!" But it's not so with God.

It was only an eleven-day journey from Egypt to Canaan (Deuteronomy 1:2), but God, in His sovereign will, purposely chose the long way. Even the long way shouldn't have taken forty years (Joshua 5:6), yet God kept rerouting the Israelites' GPS. They went into a pattern of circling in the wilderness for four decades. I'm sure you've seen value in taking a longer route to reach a destination because you wanted to avoid an accident or construction or bypass heavy traffic, but I doubt you'd ever choose a forty-year detour. What could possibly be beneficial about forty years instead of eleven days?

The shortest distance between two points is a straight line, as geometry teaches us, but God isn't a straight-line God. Sometimes He chooses the crooked path down the long and winding road because His timing is not our timing. We want shortcuts, but God knows that a good thing, or the best thing for us, may take more time.

Timing is of the essence. There are things God wants us to endure and places He wants us to spend some time. Certain seasons must last longer than others because God is up to something specific in that season. When it seems He has chosen a way that's taking a longer amount of time than you think necessary, be prepared for it to last even longer before His purposes are accomplished!

We can trust that God's timing in leading us from one point to the next is impeccable. Remember: we don't know what awaits us around the next bend, but God does!

Timing is a recurring theme in the Scriptures. In Genesis 22, Abraham was supposed to offer up his only son, Isaac, as a sacrifice. God let Abraham go through all of the motions—making a four-day journey, preparing the altar, and putting his son on it. It was only as Abraham raised the knife that God told Abraham not to kill Isaac.

In the book of Joshua, when the Israelites fought the Amorites, God made the sun stand still in the sky for about a day so the Israelites would be completely victorious over their enemies (Joshua 10:13). God isn't bound by time the way we are. If He can make the sun stand still, we can be confident that He will move in our circumstances according to His own timing.

In the New Testament, too, we see that God has a way with timing. When Lazarus fell ill in Bethany, his sisters, Martha and Mary, sent word to Jesus, who was their friend. Though Jesus had time to get to Bethany to heal Lazarus, His good friend, He purposely waited for Lazarus to die before He showed up. When Jesus finally went to Bethany, Martha and Mary were no doubt confused and upset because they knew that He could have saved their brother if He had arrived sooner (John 11:21, 32).

Yet Jesus told Martha, "Your brother will rise again" (John 11:23). Then He had the mourners roll away the stone from Lazarus's grave and told the dead man to come out. Lazarus, who had died, walked out of the grave. (We'll revisit the story of Lazarus in Chapter Four.) Jesus had delayed, allowing His friend to die before healing him, so that He could build the faith of His followers in the process. On the surface, this might seem like an insensitive, even cruel, act. How could Jesus choose to delay His arrival for the purpose of allowing Lazarus to die?

The answer: God works in His own time and His own

way, using time to His advantage. Time is a slave to the will of God!

In his letter to the Galatians, Paul explained that God sent His Son to the earth "when the set time had fully come" (Galatians 4:4). God waited for things to come together perfectly, in exactly the right set of circumstances, before He sent His Christ to us. He is doing the same in your life now: using time to His advantage and for your benefit.

If you're wondering whether the change you're waiting for will come, God may simply be saying, "It's not time yet." Maybe you're wondering how long you'll be sick or how long He expects you to stay in your current job. You may be weary of lingering in a state of uncertainty, facing a particular dilemma, carrying a particular burden, or enduring a particular trial. When God is ready, He will move. You just have to keep walking, putting one foot in front of the other, as you trust His holy GPS!

God knows what He is doing and remembers His plan for you. He didn't take Israel out of Egypt just so they could stay in the wilderness. Through all the forty years of Israel's waiting and wandering, God had Canaan in view, and He remembers the land of promise He intends for you as well. Like Israel, you may see only the rough, dry terrain, the scarcity of food, and the bitter water. But God sees quail and manna from heaven (Exodus 16) and refreshing water from a rock. No, the wilderness isn't Canaan, but God works in the wilderness.

There were no shortcuts to Canaan, and there are no shortcuts for you, either, because God knows that the journey is as important as the destination. Arriving prepared is more important than arriving soon. There's such a thing as "too early," like when you take a cake out of the oven before it's finished baking—and it sinks in the middle. How many times has your anticipation gotten the best of you in a situation? I'm so glad for the times in my life when God hasn't let me open up the oven too early!

Praise God for all the times He keeps us from short-circuiting our own destiny out of our lack of patience or knowledge. Let's be thankful that He holds our future in His capable hands.

GOD USES YOUR JOURNEY TO PREPARE YOU

Like with His timing, God is intentional about the terrain He wants us to travel through, like He picked the way of the desert and the Red Sea for the Israelites leaving Egypt. We like to choose how to get from point A to point B in our lives, and usually we like to take the fastest route, especially if our destiny at point B seems more attractive to us than where we currently are. But *God uses the journey to prepare us for the destination.*

In our hearts and minds, we attach a lot to our destiny; we tend to connect it with fulfillment. It's a place where all the aspects of our lives come together and finally make sense. We think that when we're in a place of destiny, we'll have overcome our struggles and trials and reached the sweet spot of life. We'll have what we've always wanted and be right where God wants us to be, in the center of His will. We'll have overcome so many things. Why wouldn't we want to get there as soon as possible?

But God uses our journey to prepare us fully for our destination. When we experience difficult things in life, God is readying us to enjoy our destiny when it's the right time. For us, as for the Israelites, the wilderness isn't about punishment; it's the terrain in which God develops us for our destiny. Even though an entire generation would perish in the wilderness, it was necessary for the nation's preparation to enter Canaan. If the nation of Israel was going to enter Canaan, it had to shed some things first—including most of the individuals who left Egypt originally (Numbers 14:29)—because otherwise the nation wouldn't survive and flourish in the promised land the way God intended. On our life journey, some parts of us need to die out or be cast aside before we reach our destination.

With that in mind, our prayer shouldn't be "Lord, when will I get there?" but, rather, "Lord, what part of me needs to die?" What patterns, attitudes, and behaviors stand between you and your destiny? What's keeping you from living up to His design for your life? Ask God what He is trying to purge from you through the difficult terrain you're traversing.

I don't know what your journey looks like. I don't know where the rough and jagged edges lie on your path. They may take the shape of divorce, unemployment, illness, or mistreatment. But I know that God is there every step of the way, and every one of those sharp, hard places has value. They're not pleasant, and we wouldn't choose such a road for ourselves, but all the difficulties will make sense once we reach our destiny. Our route comes out of the omniscience of God—His thoughts, not our thoughts, and His ways, not our ways. In every detail of the course of your journey, He is preparing you for the destination.

When it seems like life doesn't make sense and you're just spinning your wheels—marking time as you take blow after blow, loss after loss—God is there, building up the muscles you'll need in your place of destiny. If the Israelites had taken the easy, quick path to Canaan, God knew they would have turned back. So take heart if God is sending you on a longer, rougher route than you'd like or keeping you from the path you want to take. He doesn't want to send you by a road where the opposition you encounter would turn you back in discouragement. He is sparing you from experiences He knows would make you throw in the towel.

Thank God for the journey He has you on, because He can see what you can't see. He knows what lies down the road and how best to save and protect you. He will preserve you as He leads you to your place of destiny. And when you finally walk into that place, you'll look back and see that the journey He led you on was the way things were meant to be. It will be that much sweeter to reach your destiny knowing what you went through to get there and that it was, after all, the best way.

I don't know what destiny will look like for you. I don't even know what it will look like for me! Maybe life hurts right now. You don't know why doors slammed in your face, why your spouse left you, why God took your loved one, or why a relationship ended the way it did. But I know that God is not done. He is real and faithful, and He is at work in your life. He will always show up for you, keeping you secure one step at a time until you reach the destiny He has lovingly planned for you.

WORKBOOK

Chapter One Questions

Question: Describe a time when you wanted a situation to go a certain way but God had a different plan. What was the outcome? How did that impact your perspective on God and His ways?

_____

_____

_____

_____

_____

_____

_____

_____

_____

Question: Have you ever experienced a time when God gave a specific direction and you either followed His guidance or ignored it? What was the outcome of your decision? What did that experience teach you?

Question: What patterns, attitudes, and behaviors stand between you and your destiny? What's keeping you from living up to God's design for your life? What might He want to purge from you through difficult terrain?

_____
_____
_____
_____
_____
_____
_____
_____
_____
_____

Action: Set aside some time to give thanks to God for the journey He has you on, the destination He is leading you toward, and His goodness to get you there His way. Allow this time of worship to fill you with faith and trust in the One who is guiding you.

Chapter One Notes

CHAPTER TWO

Setbacks, Setups, and Comebacks

But Joseph said to them, "Don't be afraid. Am I in the place of God? You intended to harm me, but God intended it for good to accomplish what is now being done, the saving of many lives. So then, don't be afraid. I will provide for you and your children." And he reassured them and spoke kindly to them.

—*Genesis 50:19–21*

If you're anything like me, you want things to go according to plan. It drives you crazy when you've laid out what seems like the perfect plan to reach your destination only to have it disrupted.

Every day, many of us try to orchestrate everything with precision. We've put everything in place in advance so that when we wake up, it will simply be a matter of setting our plan in motion. Since we've already laid our clothes out, we get dressed quickly, make our first cup of coffee, and have our morning devotion. We expect the day go smoothly because we took the time to plan.

Only, something gets in the way. Maybe it's a phone call, an email, a family member bursting into the room with the latest crisis, or suddenly remembering a crucial task that slipped our mind. Whatever the specifics, sooner or later, our "perfect" plan always goes off track.

One Sunday a few years ago, I was scheduled to preach in Fort Worth, Texas. The morning before, I had to drive back home from a week of teaching in Pontiac, Michigan, just in time to prepare for an afternoon flight out of Grand Rapids. The timing was tight. I knew I'd have to throw some things in a bag, get a quick haircut, and head to the airport. But on the drive home from Pontiac, I realized that my driver's license had expired, which was a problem if I wanted to get on an airplane.

Panicked, I decided to forgo the haircut and head to the licensing office instead, where the parking lot made me wonder if we were hosting the Super Bowl and someone forgot to tell me. There were so many people there that I immediately knew I wasn't going to make my afternoon flight. Things hadn't gone according to plan.

Joseph knew something about plans going awry. Beginning in chapter 35, the book of Genesis tells his story. Joseph's life was a life filled with promise. He was his father Jacob's favorite child, the first son of Jacob's favorite wife. Yes, "favorite wife"—that should be our first clue that this was a family filled with all kinds of problems and dysfunction.

One of the problems was that Joseph knew he was his daddy's favorite, and he pranced around, flaunting this act in front of his ten half-brothers. Eventually, these older brothers grew so disgusted that they faked Joseph's death and sold him into slavery in Egypt (Genesis 37:12–36), where he wound up in prison for a crime he didn't commit (Genesis 39).

Life has way of interrupting our plans, taking us through twists, turns, peaks, and valleys that we have no way of accounting for in advance. We see this in the life of Joseph and in our own lives. Though God gave free will to us, there is always tension between our will, plans, and desires and His sovereign will. He does what He wants to, and sometimes the sovereign will of God doesn't make sense to us in the moment. His will doesn't always align with ours. Sometimes it hurts. It can involve conflict and anxiety.

There is tension between our will and God's, but ultimately, His will reigns supreme throughout the world. He is always at work behind the scenes. In every step of Joseph's problem-filled journey, through every betrayal and setback, God was there, making sure that Joseph would end up in the right place at the right time.

Even as he spent years in a cell, Joseph trusted that God had a plan for him. Eventually, Joseph went from prison to becoming Pharaoh's prime minister (Genesis 41:39–43). God literally moved him from the pit to the palace! When famine came to that part of the world, Joseph's brothers traveled to Egypt, which had enough food stored up because of Joseph's stewardship. They ended up in front of Joseph, though they didn't recognize him anymore. Joseph's brothers would never have guessed that the person they would have to appeal to for food would be the younger brother they'd sold into slavery out of jealousy all those years ago (Genesis 42:1–5). God had planned for all of this.

At the climax of the story, Joseph's brothers stood before him, his identity revealed to them (Genesis 45:1–4). Their brother was alive—and they were horrified, imagining what he might do to them. After all, he'd had decades to plot his revenge for their betrayal!

Instead, Joseph told his brothers not to be scared (Genesis 45:5). He explained that, in the end, God's good intentions outweighed their evil intentions. God used their actions to help Joseph instead of hurting him. Life is filled with setbacks, but God has a way to use them to set us up for a comeback.

SETBACKS ARE INEVITABLE

Setbacks happen to all of us, no matter how good, smart, skilled, beautiful or handsome, wealthy, or healthy we are. It's not a matter of *if*, but of *when*, because *setbacks are inevitable*. Trouble and tragedy know where we live, and setbacks come for us all, often when we least expect them. Life is filled with disruptions, like losing a job, an unexpected health diagnosis, a sudden divorce, or an unwanted pregnancy. No one is exempt from trouble in life, no matter what we have or haven't prayed for, hoped for, or accounted for. Jesus told us, "In this world you will have trouble. But take heart! I have overcome the world" (John 16:33).

Setbacks are the unavoidable consequence of sin in this fallen world. Don't let anyone convince you that because you know Jesus, you won't have trouble. Don't let anyone tell you that because you're the head and not the tail, trouble won't find you. You can get a headache while you're ahead, and your salvation won't insulate you from trouble any more than money will.

Remember how I had that trip to Forth Worth planned out to the minute, yet it fell apart because of one snag? I still might have made my flight if there hadn't been such a long line to get my license renewed. I had no control over how many people would go to the licensing office that morning. We encounter such reminders every day that we don't control our circumstances, which means there are some problems we simply cannot handle on our own.

Since setbacks will come our way, we do ourselves a disservice if we get upset with God, think He has forgotten us, or complain that life isn't fair every time we experience a setback: "God, how could You let this happen?"

Don't assume that because you've had a setback, God has walked away from you and Satan is running amok in your life. It probably has nothing to do with the devil and everything to do with what God has planned for you.

SETBACKS LEAD TO SETUPS

God is at work even in our setbacks. Sometimes God has to order up a setback to get you to your next season. If you had it your way, you would never choose trouble or trauma, but pressing through adversity is how you grow. Consider your seasons of struggle as spiritual weight training. Muscles are built by adding resistance and repetition. Any of us can think of an infinite number of activities more pleasant than weight training, but they probably would not be as effective at developing our muscles.

Setbacks lead to setups. None of us is clever, quick, slick, or agile enough to dodge a setback. If God wants it to happen, it's going to happen—but that isn't a bad thing! Don't imagine that you can be blessed only in fair weather, because God blesses us in storms, too.

In fact, in nature, something special happens during thunderstorms. God uses storms for productive ecological activity, as lightning helps turn nitrogen in the atmosphere into a form that plants (and the humans and animals that eat the plants) can absorb.[4] As surely as God uses lightning to help grass and plants grow, He can use the difficult storms of life to help you grow spiritually.

Of course, nobody is praying to God to light up the sky with lightning so terrible it makes us turn off the TV and hide under the covers. No one prays for storms of trouble, either. Yet God knows when the grass needs a lightning storm, and He knows when you need one, too, to get to the next season in your life. And so, here comes your lightning!

James said this ought to bring us joy:

> *Consider it pure joy, my brothers and sisters, whenever you face trials of many kinds, because you know that the testing of your faith produces perseverance.*
> **—James 1:2–3**

God is up to something. He is setting us up for something new. The things that happen to us unfold according to God's plan.

When Joseph's brothers faced him at last, they were bracing for a reckoning. Realizing the gravity of what they'd done to Joseph all those years before and knowing that their families' survival was now dependent on him, they were probably prepared to submit themselves to slavery. Surely, the chickens had come home to roost! But Joseph knew that God, in His sovereign will, sometimes allows us to experience bad things, so he told his brothers not to be afraid. Joseph trusted God.

It's a waste of time to ask God why the bottom has fallen out of your life. It's a waste of time to try to hold Him accountable, putting His feet to the fire, because you're going through something different and difficult.

Now, mind you, God doesn't have a problem with you expressing your frustration or disappointment with what you're going through; it doesn't diminish His will or disrupt His plan for you one bit. Your resistance simply might not get very far. David, in a fit of depression, cried out, "How long, LORD? Will you forget me forever? How long will you hide your face from me? How long must I wrestle with my thoughts and day after day have sorrow in my heart? How long will my enemy triumph over me?" (Psalm 13:1–2). God didn't say anything.

Paul wrote, "I was given a thorn in my flesh, a messenger of Satan, to torment me. Three times I pleaded with the Lord to take it away from me" (2 Corinthians 12:7–8). But instead of taking away Paul's affliction, the Lord answered, "My grace is sufficient for you, for my power is made perfect in weakness" (2 Corinthians 12:9). Paul did not pray just three prayers or on three separate occasions. The expression "three times I pleaded" implies that this was a running request Paul made, and it seemed like his requests were falling on deaf ears. Have you ever felt like God was ignoring your cry for help?

In the garden of Gethsemane, Jesus Himself, in the final hours before His death on the cross, prayed, "My Father, if it is possible, may this cup be taken from me. Yet not as I will, but as you will" (Matthew 26:39). The Father said nothing to relieve His own Son, who was carrying the sin of the world for us. Yet Jesus, by His own words, understood that the will of God is sovereign, and the Son submitted Himself to the plans of the Father.

God uses our trouble, our drama, our blemished parts, our foul pieces, and our rough edges to get us where He intends us to be. He did this for Joseph and for Joseph's brothers. Though Joseph's brothers wove their plans to destroy him, God took over those plans for His own purposes, weaving His perfect tapestry out of their corrupt cloth.

No one's life is a homogenous work of art, unchanging throughout; there are many shifts and variations. There are broken places and smooth places, dull and shiny spots, jagged and finished edges. But God makes a single piece out of all of it. You're here today, in the place where you are in your relationship with God, because of a combination of the unpleasant and the pleasant experiences in your life. A person may be wearing a brand-new suit, but it's hiding some scars.

If you think that other people have succeeded in ruining

you, it's time to exchange your ashes for "a crown of beauty" (Isaiah 61:3) because God has a plan to use what those people have done to you to get you where He wants you to be, like He did for Joseph. What they did and what happened to you hurt, and it still hurts, but God allowed it for a reason. He allowed it for your benefit.

God is using your setback to set you up, so buckle up! In His perfect timing, God will drive you up out of the valley to the next mountaintop in your life. The road will take you through the fire, and your past may be hot on your tail, trying to run you down. But you can trust God to get you to your destination, even if He tells you to get out of the car and take a sidewalk through the sea. Joseph's road took him through years of slavery and prison, yet look where the journey ended: the palace, where he gave the orders and was the one being served.

When life has thrown someone down on the mat and everyone is counting him or her out, we love to see that person rise up and keep fighting. Joseph's brothers had counted him out long ago, but God used their evil actions for his deliverance and theirs.

If life is pushing against you today, keep on pushing back, like you'd push through physical training. Push through those spiritual sit-ups! Keep on praying, praising, and trusting. There's always a comeback.

GOD IS POSITIONING YOU

Remember that *life is about positioning*. The enemy weaves, but so does God. God has a plan to get you from your current position to your next position. What looks like death, divorce, prison, or a pink slip right now looks like something entirely different, and better, from God's perfect vantage point. If doors start closing all around you, thank God for keeping you away from dead ends. And when He opens up a window for you, jump through it to your next experience! No matter how difficult the journey has been, how vicious the attacks against you, or how lacking you think you are in qualifications and resources, He will provide you strength, sustenance, and everything else you require every step of your journey.

This is how Paul could say, in Romans 8:28, that God works all things for our good. It's how the prophets, like Isaiah, could speak of God taking broken things and redeeming them for something better and beautiful. The trickery and sinfulness of man is no match for God's plans! Abraham was a liar who became the father of our faith. Paul once persecuted followers of Jesus, but God used him like no other to spread the gospel. Joseph was a spoiled, proud young man whom God used to show mercy to his dysfunctional family and feed whole nations.

God has a way of taking all your troubles, disappointments, and broken pieces and making something beautiful out of your life. He already has a plan!

WORKBOOK

Chapter Two Questions

Question: Think of a time when you planned things to go a certain way but your plans got derailed. How did you react to that curveball? Did your reaction help or hinder the situation? In hindsight, how would you handle the situation differently?

_____

_____

_____

_____

_____

_____

_____

Question: Have you ever thought that something was a setback but later discovered that it was a useful part of God's broader plan? Why is it challenging to keep that perspective in the middle of difficult circumstances? What steps can you take to practice trusting in God's plan in all situations and areas of your life?

Question: Is something in your life right now pushing you to your breaking point? What do you think God wants to show you through this situation? How can you change your thoughts about it to be in alignment with God's faithfulness?

_____

_____

_____

_____

_____

_____

_____

_____

_____

_____

Action: If you're feeling tapped out, there is Someone you can turn to for strength and sustenance. Spend quality time with God, inviting Him to give you what you need to make it through this difficult season. Open your heart to all He wants to teach you. In a notebook or journal, write down anything God brings to your mind that offers you hope and encouragement.

Chapter Two Notes

CHAPTER THREE

It's Not What It Looks Like

> *This is what the* LORD *says: "When seventy years are completed for Babylon, I will come to you and fulfill my good promise to bring you back to this place. For I know the plans I have for you," declares the* LORD, *"plans to prosper you and not to harm you, plans to give you hope and a future."*
> —*Jeremiah 29:10–11*

When we are on our way to the place God wants us to be, there will be seasons and episodes that don't quite seem to add up. They don't seem logical.

Our natural assumption is that our journey of becoming the people God intends ought to be a clear-cut progression, like rounding the bases on a baseball diamond: first base, second base, third base, home. But the process of "becoming" is not so simple and straightforward. We can make it to second base only to be sent back to first. Sometimes third base feels like being back on first base.

I'm sure you can recall seasons of your journey that have

been messy and confusing. Maybe you're experiencing such a season right now. "Becoming" doesn't always look pretty or feel easy, especially when it involves loss, grief, or other hardship, which often happens for reasons outside our control. Even if we dot every *i* and cross every *t*, the bottom can still fall out of our situation. The truth is that life doesn't always make sense. Being a Christian and trusting God don't always feel wholesome or look like grace or make you want to shout, "Hallelujah!"

The prophet Jeremiah spoke on God's behalf to the Israelite nation of Judah, which King Nebuchadnezzar of Babylon was about to conquer. The people of Judah, removed from their beloved city of Jerusalem, their temple destroyed, would recall the prophet's words of judgment during the years of their captivity in Babylon. The kingdom of Judah was God's chosen people, representatives of His grace in the world, yet they suddenly found themselves enslaved to a heathen empire. It made no sense. But through Jeremiah, God declared that He had a plan.

Though we may not be exiled or enslaved, there can still be an element of captivity in our lives. Hardships, negative thinking, or lies can hold us captive if we allow them to. Nothing has the power to paralyze and restrict us like distorted thoughts and opinions. We can be imprisoned by the negative thoughts we generate ourselves or by internalizing others' negative attitudes toward us.

At face value, some seasons of our lives look hopeless, which can make us susceptible to the lies that God is not active in our lives and does not care about us. When you find yourself in such a season, hold on because it's not what it looks like!

THIS SEASON WON'T LAST FOREVER

Remember that *there are seasons on your journey to becoming, and they're of limited duration.* It's not a straightforward, consistent, or clean process; rather, it's jagged, topsy-turvy, and messy. There will be seasons of hardship, in which success seems elusive, you cannot change your circumstances, and you feel stuck in a narrative of disappointment. Other people might not seem to care about you, and God might not seem to remember you or respond to your prayers.

Of course, He does remember you, and He has designed the seasons in your life to have parameters, or limits. Even if it seems like God will not make things better than they are, He has an end in sight for your present trouble. No matter your situation, however heavy or dark or frustrating it feels, God has planned an end to it. You won't be spinning your wheels or marking time indefinitely.

As mentioned in Chapter One, our rational selves crave an explanation for everything: "Why, God? Why do I have to go through this?" I can't tell you why you're going through hardship, but I can assure you that God has the answers. He knows why you're in your current season and how long you need to be there. The fact that He knows these things ought to be good enough for us if we say that we trust Him. Instead of pushing back against God, complaining that we don't like our situation, or protesting its unfairness, we ought to open ourselves to what He wants to do in our lives right now, in these circumstances. Trust Him on your journey to becoming and know that any season of trouble has a set duration.

God has the perfect vantage point to see the parameters of our seasons because He is an eternal God. Your joy isn't tied to your circumstances but to a mighty, wise God who exists outside of the constraints of time and is always faithful to take care of His children. He will make good on His promises, even if it's not in the way or the time you expect. You can trust His "plans to prosper you and not to harm you, plans to give you hope and a future" (Jeremiah 29:11). Because of this, you can have joy even in one of life's downpours or a season of loss.

It's telling that I don't hear any prophets today saying, "In twenty-one days, you're going to have a terrible accident and wind up in the hospital," "You will lose your home in a fire," "Your business will fail," or anything along those lines. The kinds of sensationalized prophecies receiving attention nowadays seem to entail some promise of supernatural gain or success. That's the sort of prophecy people's itching ears want to hear, but much of the time, God's plans work differently. Difficult seasons are a scriptural reality!

King Solomon of Israel, known for his wisdom, said:

> There is a time for everything, and a season for every activity under the heavens: a time to be born and a time to die, a time to plant and a time to uproot, a time to kill and a time to heal, a time to tear down and a time to build, a time to

> weep and a time to laugh, a time to mourn and a time to dance....
> —Ecclesiastes 3:1–4

When you find yourself in a hard place, remind yourself that it's only for a season. Though this might be your season for hardship, all of the seasons God has planned for you are productive for your good.

GOD KNOWS YOUR FUTURE IN FULL DETAIL

God has total and exclusive access to knowledge of what lies ahead for us. *Our future is disclosed fully to Him.* "*I* know the plans I have for you," He said to Jeremiah (Jeremiah 29:11, emphasis mine). The subtext of this declaration is that other people may profess to know God's plans, but He alone knows what He has in store for each of us. Though all kinds of people may want to weigh in on your circumstances and speak into your life, God is the only expert.

That won't stop some people from claiming to be experts on your life. We all know them: those individuals who act like they know everything about everyone's life, except maybe their own. They like to tell you things like when you should leave your job or your spouse.

"What you need to do is...."

"You ought to...."

"You know, I was thinking about you the other day. You should...."

Amid all the chaos and confusion of their lives, these

fountains of unsolicited advice go out of their way to tell you what to do in your situation. Why don't they take their own advice and apply their supposed expertise to their own lives? Before they tell you what job you ought to have, maybe they should get a job!

By contrast, God really knows what your path looks like, in full detail, and *only* He knows. In Jeremiah's time, false prophets claimed to understand the times, to foresee what lay in store for God's people, and to know what was best for the kingdom of Judah. Through Jeremiah, God asserted that He alone knew all these things.

It is a fundamental truth that God has total vision and perfect clarity about our lives. He knows what He is doing and why because the master plan belongs to Him. You can build your life according to your preferred plan all you want, but no matter how much energy you expend, your plan will always be subservient to the will of God. He knows His plan and your plan, so He knows the difference. Accordingly, we serve ourselves best by trying to match our plans with God's plan instead of trying to align ourselves with someone else's ideas for us or about us.

For similar reasons, be careful with the comparison game. Don't assume you're doing something wrong just because you don't have what someone else has. If other people seem further along in their journeys than you are or their paths seems smoother, it's not because you messed up or missed something. God has a different plan for each person. Besides, you don't have full knowledge of other people's journeys, and you don't even know if they're in line with God's intentions for their lives!

Our only wise and sensible option is to surrender to the plan of God, "the author and finisher of our faith" (Hebrews 12:2 NKJV). Don't rely on your own understanding, but "in all your ways submit to him, and he will make your paths straight" (Proverbs 3:5–6). For the word of God "is a lamp for my feet, a light on my path" (Psalm 119:105). Do you want to understand the will of God for your life? Then consult His Word! Otherwise, you will always be stumbling through life by trial and error, and no one can afford to live that way.

With the words of prophecy God gave Jeremiah, He reassured a nation in captivity and exile, saying, in effect, "It's all going according to plan, and that plan won't harm you." Now, that sounds contradictory to the circumstances God's people were in, and it may sound contradictory to your situation today. If God's plan is not meant to harm us, why does it hurt sometimes? The truth is that it hurts to be laid off, to be left alone, or to be sick with no relief in sight. If we're following what seems to be His plan, we feel that we ought to experience some sort of advancement or progress. As loving as God is, there is no exemption from pain.

But it is also true that we don't know everything. God knows what's happening behind the scenes in our lives in a way we're not privy to. When we watch a movie, we view each scene from only one perspective at a time, and we can't see the crews moving around cameras, lighting, and sets. We don't see the writers working on the script, the composer working on the score, or the editors adding sounds and effects. We don't see all the footage left on the cutting-room floor. But God, the director of our lives, sees it all.

If you're in one of life's storms, be encouraged that God knows how big the cloud overhead needs to be and how long you need to delay in the downpour. Fill out all the job applications you want, but God knows how long your résumé needs to sit in employers' inboxes before you get a call. He knows how to tie up your job search until the perfect time for you to experience a change. Though confusion can hurt, God is always at work to prosper you, even when you're sleeping, waiting, feeling rejected, or staring a closed door in the face. God might shut all the doors in front of you so that when the timing is right, you'll see the side door or window He has opened. No matter what happens in front of you, God is working behind the scenes on your behalf.

Maybe that dream job you desire would make you miserable; maybe that company you've applied to is about to fold suddenly. Instead, out of the blue, your current job that you think is a dead end might unexpectedly lead to a promotion. Only God knows because only He has all the information—a full, panoramic view.

GOD HAS A UNIQUE PLAN FOR YOU

If someone comes up to you and tells you that he or she knows God's plan for you, say, "Thanks, but He will let me know in His good time." *God has a specific, unique plan for you based on His omniscient, all-encompassing knowledge of your journey.*

What most people in the kingdom of Judah failed to realize was that God used Babylon to defeat them and take them captive to get them to the next season of their relationship with Him. God allowed His people to suffer and be enslaved, but it was all according to His plan. The enemies of Judah captured Jerusalem, carried off the best and brightest young men (Jeremiah 24:1), and looted and burned Solomon's temple (2 Kings 25), depriving God's people of their religious institutions. But none of these devastating events were what they looked like.

Though the bottom may seem to be falling out of your life, your journey is not random; it's methodical. God uses your hardship, like Romans 8:28 says He uses everything, for your greater good. Whatever you're going through now might not look or feel or smell good, but it's always *for* your good. Even when you're broken, God is still blessing you! It's not the way you wanted things to happen, any more than Abraham wanted to tie up his son on the altar and raise the knife before God sent the ram to sacrifice in Isaac's place. But God had a plan, the best plan, for Abraham's journey, and He made sure the ram was coming all along.

You can't see everything God is doing in your life, and it's not time for you to know yet. But if you're ready to run, to quit, or to walk out today, be confident that God is already on the case. His plan is in the works, and He has a hope and a future lined up for you. Like a child who believes implicitly what his father says, trust that God knows what He is talking about. Believe Him when He says that He has your future arranged and when He says that He will show up to bring you to your destination. It might take longer than you want, but He will get there. In fact, He is already there. He just hasn't revealed Himself yet.

The hope God spoke of through Jeremiah was no ordinary hope; it was a messianic hope beyond anything the people of Judah imagined. They'd lost their religious traditions, but a messiah would come to fill the void. Jesus would come as their high priest, conquering king, and deliverer. He would give them an eternal hope and future against which the chains and armies of the Babylonians were powerless.

God's plans are bigger than your sickness, hardship, and loss. No matter what the present looks like, your future looks bright because Christ has already come! The future is glorious for us, and it is already completely assured.

WORKBOOK

Chapter Three Questions

Question: In what ways (if any) are you trusting and relying upon a "perfect" plan to bring you a sense of security and stability more than you are relying on God's faithfulness, promises, and guidance? How is your reliance upon your plan hindering your faith? How can you shift your trust toward God?

_____

_____

_____

_____

_____

_____

_____

_____

_____

_____

_____

Question: What is your attitude when things don't go the way you want them to or how you think they should? Does your response line up with your professed trust in God?

_____

_____

_____

_____

_____

_____

_____

_____

_____

_____

Question: Have you ever received unsolicited advice that contradicted what God was revealing to you? How difficult did you find it to reject the advice?

_____

_____

_____

_____

_____

_____

_____

_____

_____

_____

Action: Do you feel like you have a clear sense of where God is guiding you, or do you need more clarity? Do you feel a sense of peace even if you are in a season of waiting, without clear direction?

Whatever it is you need in this moment to be anchored and rooted in God, spend some time communicating that to Him. Look up Bible verses that can bring a sense of peace and hope when the situations around you seem chaotic. Write them on paper or notecards, or print them out and refer to them when you are struggling to have peace.

Chapter Three Notes

CHAPTER FOUR

The Ministry of Delay

So the sisters sent word to Jesus, "Lord, the one you love is sick."

When he heard this, Jesus said, "This sickness will not end in death. No, it is for God's glory so that God's Son may be glorified through it." Now Jesus loved Martha and her sister and Lazarus. So when he heard that Lazarus was sick, he stayed where he was two more days, and then he said to his disciples, "Let us go back to Judea."

—*John 11:3–7*

I remember my first band trip, in my freshman year of high school. Band trips at my high school were legendary! After hearing the stories of excitement and fun, I couldn't wait to experience it all for myself.

We were scheduled to go to Nashville, Tennessee. All of the band students and their parents had gathered in the band room, and you could feel the excitement and energy in the air. We all had our clothes, pillows, blankets, and instruments, as well as comic books or headphones to keep entertained on the ride since those were the days before cell phones, tablets, and social media.

We were ready to say goodbye to our parents for the scheduled departure at 6 p.m., but our bus hadn't arrived yet. The clock hit 6:05, 6:15, and 6:30, with no sign of the bus. Parents started to leave, saying that we should call them when we arrived in Nashville. When 8 p.m. rolled around with no bus in sight, it was getting dark outside, and I asked my band director, "Are we still going to go?"

"Oh yes," he assured me. But when?

We moved outside the band room to wait, as if that would prompt the bus to get there faster. We brought all our stuff with us and piled it up on the sidewalk, waiting expectantly. We knew that our transportation should be there by now.

At 9:30 p.m., we retreated back inside the band room, took out our pillows, and found spots where we could curl up to sleep.

Sometime between 10:30 and 11 p.m., someone finally called out, "Bus!" But there was no excitement anymore. We dragged ourselves outside, threw our belongings under the bus, and made the trek to Nashville.

Nobody likes interruptions to their plans or when things don't go as desired. We anticipate our next season with excitement, looking for something grand, and when this doesn't happen because of delays, we're disappointed and upset. In those moments, no explanation or reasoning will console us. Nothing would have made me feel better about losing out on nearly five hours of my first band trip.

In Chapter One, I mentioned the story of Lazarus (John

11) as an example of how God uses time to His advantage and for His purposes. Jesus' good friend Lazarus had fallen ill, and His presence was requested by Mary and Martha. We all identify with Mary and Martha in their desperation. Rather than share their sense of urgency, Jesus intentionally waited before He made His way to their house in Bethany.

In His delay, we see that having a relationship with Jesus does not exempt us from our earthly troubles. While delay heightens our anxiety, it poses no urgency or threat to Him. Even though Jesus did not come when they wanted Him to come, He still performed a miracle, which shows that His delay in our lives does not mean denial.

Though no one likes to be delayed, there is, in fact, a ministry in God's delays. Jesus knew that Lazarus was sick but purposely waited for him to die. He didn't hurry. In this, God was up to something. He has a way of using delays, painful though they may be, to be productive in our lives and help us grow. If you've got your bags packed for the next season but things aren't shaping up the way you expected, God hasn't forgotten you. Have you asked God what He wants to show or teach you in your season of waiting?

DELAY DOES NOT DISCRIMINATE

Though Mary, Martha, and Lazarus were Jesus' good friends and He loved them, He didn't give in and rush God's plan. Why not? Simply put, *delay does not discriminate.*

Once when I was traveling by air, I was checking in at the gate and waiting to board the flight when someone announced on the intercom that the flight was delayed. You could hear the collective sigh of frustration at the gate. It was like my freshman-year band trip all over again!

I wasn't in a particular hurry on this occasion because I was traveling for leisure, but I saw people in business suits tugging on their ties anxiously. Other travelers spoke agitatedly on their phones. However, the delay didn't ask for their permission, and their anxiety didn't change anything.

Likewise, when God has planned a delay, He won't check in with you first to see if you think you need it! It didn't matter that Lazarus and his sisters were special to Jesus. The tension in this narrative lies between the moment Jesus received news of His beloved friend's illness and the fact that He purposely waited after hearing this report from Bethany. He waited two extra days even though, as Scripture says, He "loved Martha and her sister and Lazarus" (John 11:5).

You may think that you're the Lord's favorite child because of your devotion in prayer, in worship, in serving, in attendance. You may think that you have an "in" with God and He will fast-track your life, always answering your prayers immediately. But if He tells you to sit, you're going to sit—and it's not because you did anything wrong.

Delay doesn't have to be your fault. God may just want to do something different from what you want. His love doesn't exempt us from waiting any more than it exempts us from earthly trouble. Just because God loves us doesn't mean we won't experience pain. Jesus tells us this in John 16:33 so we can have hope, as surely as He tells us that He has overcome the world.

I know that as long as you live, you'll love the Lord and you'll love other people, but you'll still cry sometimes because delay does not discriminate. There's no fast track or TSA per-check line with God. We can't all be first-class Christian flyers all the time. Sometimes we have to fly coach.

Perhaps a question to ponder in our periods of waiting is how we can be productive during such seasons. There's nothing productive in throwing a tantrum.

YOUR URGENCY DOESN'T AFFECT GOD'S DELAY

Lazarus was so sick that his sisters knew their local physician wouldn't be able to heal him. But they had a friend in Jesus, who was a healer, and they'd seen Him in action! If He could open the eyes of the blind, He could heal Lazarus, all the more because He loved them—right?

But that's not how it happened, because *God's timing and delays are not subject to our perceptions of urgency.* Lazarus died, though Jesus said, "This sickness will not end in death" (John 11:4).

Martha and Mary might not have had the knowledge, skill, or acumen to diagnose Lazarus, but they knew it was serious. The messenger must have raced from their home to Jesus as fast as he could so Jesus could hurry to Bethany and save Lazarus. But Jesus was chilling. He didn't take everyone else's urgency as His urgency. He didn't raise His voice or tell His disciples to get a move on. Yes, He acknowledged the seriousness of Lazarus's condition, but then He took His time because, in this case, He preferred for His friend to die. On the face of it, that's troubling!

We assume that God will feel the urgency we feel about our situation. We feel desperate, so we're certain that He must act decisively and soon in our circumstances, but God chooses to take His time anyway. We fast and pray and study and strategize, burning the midnight oil to try to get a plan in place and moving, because if something doesn't change in our life, we're not sure how long we can stand it. And still, God takes His time. Why?

Jesus waited until Lazarus died before coming to Bethany because He knew that was the best way to glorify God. Though Lazarus died, God was always in control of the situation.

On a previous occasion, when Jesus and the disciples were crossing the Sea of Galilee to meet Jesus and a storm came upon them, the disciples were terrified—and Jesus had the audacity to take a nap. Our urgency doesn't translate into urgency for God. Nowhere in Scripture does God hurry. Not once does He share in the consternation or frantic behavior of His children. There's no need, because He is never at a loss and is always in control.

In fact, God's control is such that He allows the trouble to be productive in our lives. He makes trouble behave, doing as He commands. He can tell a storm exactly how long to rage in our lives before He tells it to stop, and it stops! He can stop the sun in the sky if He wants to.

Still, we identify more with Martha and Mary than with Jesus. We would have shared in their confusion when Jesus said that Lazarus's sickness would not end in death. And we would have shared the disciples' dismay when Jesus slept while the storm threatened to overturn their boat. We want to cry out to God, "When are we going to leave? When will we get there?" And He tells us, "Soon enough."

DELAY IS NOT DENIAL

I don't know where in your life it feels like God has put you in a holding pattern, slowing time and making you wait. It's not up to me or you to decide if it's been long enough, though I'm sure you feel like it's been long enough. But I assure you that *being delayed is not being denied*.

After all, Jesus got the message. He acknowledged that it was a dire situation for Lazarus, even though He chose to delay instead of responding the way others expected. He recognized others' urgency as an opportunity to glorify the Father. God will take your life and use it as a stage to stand on to do great work.

Consider Job, who was a righteous man Satan wanted to destroy. God and Satan had a conversation about Job, and God decided to let Satan go to work in the life of this man who loved God (Job 1:6–12). We wouldn't expect God to offer us up to Satan, but that's what He did with Job, only specifying that Satan wasn't allowed to kill him.

Then the bottom fell out of Job's life as he lost his children, his riches, and his health to the point where his wife told him to "curse God and die" (Job 2:9). His friends told him that he must be doing something wrong. Nonetheless, God used Job's adversity as a stage to bless him.

God can likewise bless you in your trials, turmoil, and pain. He will show up when He is ready. I know the wait has been too long, the load too heavy, but God will show up when He needs to show up—and that might be when you feel like you're just about to break, and a little longer still.

People assumed that Jesus had to be present while Lazarus was still alive if He was going to heal His friend, but Lazarus had already died when Jesus finally arrived. Everyone was assuming that God had limits He did not, which accounted for their urgency. They assumed that Jesus needed to hurry, but God was ready to take His miracles to a whole other level. They'd seen Him turn water to wine and heal the sick and the blind, but they hadn't yet seen Him conquer death. It was time for Jesus to stand on a bigger stage and show people what they'd never seen before.

When God seems to be taking His time in your life, it could be because He is waiting to show you something you've never seen before. As you wait, just imagine how much glory God will reveal in your life. You're tired, but you know He will show up. It doesn't matter what your family, your friends, your boss, your coworkers, your doctors, or your lawyers have said; God knows where you are and what you need. When He shows up in your life, He can roll the stone back on a dead dream, a dead marriage, or a dead career. He can stand outside the grave, what seems like four days too late, and say, "Lazarus, come out!" (John 11:43). No coroner's report or laws of nature can keep Lazarus in the grave when that happens.

Like Lazarus, it's time to hop out of the grave and "take

off the grave clothes" (John 11:44)—dusting off that pipe dream, opportunity, or relationship God gave you but you gave up for dead—because God isn't finished working yet.

God may not come or act when we want Him to, but because He is not bound by the same constraints as we are, He is able to care for us in ways only He can. God does the impossible. He "is able to do immeasurably more than all we ask or imagine, according to his power that is at work within us" (Ephesians 3:20). God is using the delays in your life for your benefit. Other people may be writing you off and counting you out, but you can count on Him to deliver!

WORKBOOK

Chapter Four Questions

Question: How do you typically respond to interruptions or delays on a small scale and on a large scale? How can your attitude about small hiccups in your daily schedule affect how you respond to seemingly big delays in your life goals?

_____
_____
_____
_____
_____
_____
_____
_____
_____

_____

_____

Question: Do you find it difficult to bless or praise God when you are experiencing trials in your life? Why do you think that is? How does equating God's favor with a prosperous or easy life hinder our ability to worship God when things get tough?

_____

_____

_____

_____

_____

_____

_____

_____

_____

Question: Describe a painful or difficult trial through which you experienced God's blessings. How did that differ from what you thought God's blessings would look like?

_____

_____

_____

_____

_____

_____

_____

_____

_____

_____

Action: Make a list of areas in your life you feel are dead or beyond hope. Spend some time expressing this to God. Ask Him to breathe life into those areas, and surrender to His timing.

Chapter Four Notes

CHAPTER FIVE

Storms as Classrooms

> *That day when evening came, he [Jesus] said to his disciples, "Let us go over to the other side." Leaving the crowd behind, they took him along, just as he was, in the boat. There were also other boats with him. A furious squall came up, and the waves broke over the boat, so that it was nearly swamped. Jesus was in the stern, sleeping on a cushion. The disciples woke him and said to him, "Teacher, don't you care if we drown?"*
>
> *He got up, rebuked the wind and said to the waves, "Quiet! Be still!" Then the wind died down and it was completely calm.*
>
> *He said to his disciples, "Why are you so afraid? Do you still have no faith?"*
>
> *They were terrified and asked each other, "Who is this? Even the wind and the waves obey him!"*
>
> —*Mark 4:35–41*

Even if we haven't experienced a hurricane in person, we've all seen images or news footage of the destruction and suffering wrought by massive storms. When my family moved to Houston in 2001, the forecast called for a tropical depression. That system intensified to a tropical storm. Just behind our home was a bayou, and we watched the water rise. Water flooded the streets; there was devastation. The highways were like lakes, with tractor trailers floating like boats. Cars piled up along the side of the road.

In August 2005, Hurricane Katrina, "the costliest natural disaster in U. S. history," hit New Orleans.[5] It wasn't necessarily the power of the storm's winds that caused the destruction, but the storm surge that broke through the levees meant to protect the city from flooding. About eighty percent of the city flooded, and ultimately, over 1,800 people died as a result of Katrina. A few weeks later, Hurricane Rita prompted many of us to evacuate Houston.

Storms turn lives upside down. They destroy homes and level trees. But there are also benefits from these phenomena.[6] Though destructive by nature, they also have productive qualities. They bring water to places that are lacking, and they help regulate temperature across the earth. They restore coastal areas by depositing new sand and nutrients and washing away or breaking up the old and stagnant. They remove weak and diseased trees, allowing forests to regenerate. Storms are a necessity to maintain and revitalize the world God created, and the storms of life do the same for us.

In part, times of trouble in our lives do this by providing an environment for God to teach us certain lessons. In other words, storms are classrooms, and Jesus is the master teacher. The winds and the rain give us something new and fresh to experience, a hands-on application of the things He wants us to learn.

The Gospels tell us about one field trip Jesus took His disciples on, into a literal storm (Mark 4:35–41; it's also found in Matthew 8 and Luke 8). Jesus instructed His disciples to set sail, knowing that the storm lay ahead, because He had a lesson in mind. Following His will led His followers into trouble, but He was with them. Our storms are subject to God's authority, and He likes to use these destructive forces to bring about some of our greatest blessings.

In other words, though devastating, storms also have productive qualities. The problem in this situation was not the storm, but the disciples' lack of faith. Jesus used the storm as an opportunity to minister to His followers about what it means to have faith in Him.

STORMS ARE INEVITABLE

A key principle we learn from this story of Jesus calming the storm is that *storms must come*. Again and again in Scripture and in our lives, we see that trials are inevitable; there are no exemptions from storms. Remember that, in John 16:33, Jesus assured us we would have trouble. You can stormproof your house, but you can't keep the storm from coming. You can Scripture up, pray up, and praise up, but you can't stop the thunder from rolling into your life.

The episode with the storm came after Jesus had been teaching the crowds with parables, or stories. There doesn't seem to have been any indication that bad weather was brewing on the Sea of Galilee, and Jesus said nothing about a storm. The disciples expected no trouble, yet the storm came anyway. The Sea of Galilee was surrounded by mountains, which created the possibility of sudden storms no one could see coming.[7]

In your life, too, there will be unexpected storms, seemingly out of nowhere. You may be sitting in the doctor's office, thinking that you just have a tickle in your throat, when the doctor comes out with a serious diagnosis. You may be sitting at a stoplight, minding your own business, when a drunk driver comes out of nowhere. Your loved one may leave you or be taken from you without warning.

Even being in the presence of Jesus Himself didn't keep the storm from coming the disciples' way! There's nothing you can do, either—no words of prayer, no way of serving in your church—to stop the onset of one of life's storms. These things may happen even if you're squarely in the middle of God's will for you, so don't blame yourself when trouble comes your way, no matter what diagnosis some people may offer about the root of your circumstances.

Storms are inevitable. You can love God faithfully and be walking alongside Him, but that won't stop the strong winds from blowing. There are no exemptions—that's the first lesson Jesus was teaching His disciples in the classroom of this storm. But at the same time, we can take heart in knowing that dark clouds don't mean God isn't there with us.

God Is With You in the Storm

The second lesson, then, was that *storms are not solitary experiences*. Jesus didn't tell His disciples, "Hey, head on over, and I'll meet you on the other side." He said, "Let us go over to the other side" (Mark 4:35).

Don't miss the pronoun "us" here. There is immense power packed into this two-letter word. It speaks to the relational character of Jesus. This is another expression of the Immanuel, or "God with us." He did not simply send them into the approaching storm, but accompanied them. The disciples had the physical presence of Jesus during the storm that followed.

Jesus didn't decide to rest on shore after preaching all day, putting the disciples in the boat and letting them fend for themselves without Him. Instead, when the disciples heeded His command and got into the boat, He was with them the whole way, and He is with you as well. Jesus takes you with Him and accompanies you through your life's journey.

Notice, however, that Jesus was asleep on the boat. Though the storm beats against you, causing a commotion in your life, your mind, and your heart, Jesus isn't worried. He showed His disciples that it was okay to rest in the storm because He was present, though they failed to understand that truth in the moment.

We all go through some real challenges, and I may be a pastor, but there are moments when I admit to God, "Lord, I don't know about this one." At times, we lack the faith, courage, and understanding to trust God, and our own negative thoughts and faulty thinking take over. We may pray, "God, I need You to show up in a hurry!"

But Jesus taught us that God is already present. He is an omnipresent God! That means we don't need to give God a self-diagnosis, assessing our situation and how we got there. These may be good things to reflect on, but God already knows it all, with greater clarity and accuracy. He is everywhere and sees everything, so He doesn't need us to bring Him up to speed. He already knows what's happened and what's needed.

CALL ON GOD IN YOUR STORM

The disciples were frantic, afraid, and doubtful whether God cared about their lives. But at this point, they showed some aptitude for the classroom experience Jesus had arranged: they at least had enough sense to wake Jesus up. In other words, they called on Him because they knew He had the power to help them.

Take a page from the disciples' book and quit trying to figure out or handle your situation on your own. *In the midst of life's storms, call on God!* You can't call too early, too loudly, or too often. Call on Him every chance you get, because you need Him every hour and He is there with you, ready to help.

Faith isn't supposed to get scared, but it happens to all of us. Jesus knows this. I'm so glad to read that He didn't punish the disciples for their lack of faith but, instead, helped them. If people were to interrupt you in the middle of a good nap, they'd probably wish they hadn't. And Jesus wasn't napping lightly, either; after all, He was sleeping through a storm! In other words, Jesus was in a deep sleep, the kind you might wake up from not knowing what day of the week it is. But when the disciples shook Jesus awake, He showed them grace and taught them by stopping the storm.

GOD IS MASTER OF THE STORM

The way Jesus brought the storm to a sudden halt emphasizes another lesson in this spiritual classroom experience: *every storm has a Master*. A storm is not an autonomous, self-governed event in your life, moving of its own accord and by its own authority. As violent and destructive as they may be, storms are on a leash. God is their Master, and He is meticulous. He will let a given storm blow down only so many trees.

We all have debris in our lives, like bad thinking and attitudes and habits, that we need a storm to clean out. When a storm has produced everything God wants it to in our lives, He will bring it to an end. Once your hurricane has transformed the way you think about the world or talk about other people or see yourself, bringing in fresh water and making room for new growth, the storm will blow over. "Weeping may stay for the night," David sang, "but rejoicing comes in the morning" (Psalm 30:5).

Jesus stopped the winds and the waves with only a brief command—"Quiet! Be still!" (Mark 4:39)—because He was its master. So hold on. God has your storm under control, and He won't let it last one second longer than it needs to. He will give you peace, "the peace of God, which transcends all understanding" (Philippians 4:7).

Yes, storms come our way. God can use them to teach us timeless principles that will nurture us on our journey. For instance, we must remember that we are never alone in them, because Jesus is always with us. We must have faith in His ability to protect us and to end our storms according to His own timing, because even the wind and water, the thunder, and the lightning obey His voice. As painful and abrasive as the hurricanes of life may feel, as inconvenient and unfair as they may seem, God uses these storms in the tenderest way to remove clutter and produce good things in our lives.

WORKBOOK

Chapter Five Questions

Question: Why do you think we need storms for us to grow? When have you experienced growth through a storm, and how did it change your perspective?

_____
_____
_____
_____
_____
_____
_____
_____
_____

Question: What can you do to prepare yourself mentally, physically, spiritually, and emotionally for the storms of life you will inevitably encounter? Are you doing any of these things already?

_____

_____

_____

_____

_____

_____

_____

_____

Question: Do you lean on Jesus and trust Him to protect you when you experience hard times? Do you need to strengthen your relationship with Him to ensure that you will stay connected to Him when you experience trials? What changes to your lifestyle would better allow God to strengthen you for storms?

_____

_____

_____

_____

_____

_____

_____

_____

_____

_____

_____

_____

Action: What difficulties have you experienced that left you unsure whether you learned or gained anything from them? Re-evaluate those circumstances from the perspective you have now. Can you see any good that came from them? Can you discover any lesson woven into these experiences?

Chapter Five Notes

CHAPTER SIX

Finding Peace in the Pieces

When daylight came, they did not recognize the land, but they saw a bay with a sandy beach, where they decided to run the ship aground if they could. Cutting loose the anchors, they left them in the sea and at the same time untied the ropes that held the rudders. Then they hoisted the foresail to the wind and made for the beach. But the ship struck a sandbar and ran aground. The bow stuck fast and would not move, and the stern was broken to pieces by the pounding of the surf.

The soldiers planned to kill the prisoners to prevent any of them from swimming away and escaping. But the centurion wanted to spare Paul's life and kept them from carrying out their plan. He ordered those who could swim to jump overboard first and get to land. The rest were to get there on planks or on other pieces of the ship. In this way everyone reached land safely.

—*Acts 27:39–44*

In 2009, Rick DeVos launched the art competition ArtPrize in Grand Rapids, Michigan. In 2011, the winning entry was called "Crucifixion," by Mia Tavonatti.[8] Standing thirteen feet tall and nine feet wide, this work of art took Tavonatti 2,500 hours to complete and weighed 425 pounds. It was a depiction of Jesus on the cross, comprising thousands of cut pieces of stained glass—one cohesive piece of art made from many small fragments.

In our journeys, too, we can have wholeness even if our lives are broken into tiny pieces. Sometimes all we have are fragments to sustain us in various seasons of our lives. One day, we feel like we have everything we need, and it all fits together neatly. Then we have experiences in our lives that shatter our places of comfort and confidence. Suddenly, we don't have the resources and the material, financial, or physical security we used to have. While the remnants of our previous life may be nothing like what we once had or imagined for ourselves, God still uses them to carry, sustain, and preserve us through our troubles.

The entire chapter of Acts 27 describes the end of Paul's ministry, when he was on his way to Rome to stand trial before the emperor. Despite Paul's warnings about sailing at that time of year, the Roman soldiers and ship's crew continued making their way across the Mediterranean Sea near Greece. With Paul and other prisoners in tow, they encountered a violent storm with hurricane-force winds. This storm kept up day after day, threatening the lives of everyone on board—so much so that they started unloading cargo and some of the sailors tried to abandon ship.

But God told Paul that everyone would make it if they all stuck with the ship, so Paul reassured the Roman soldiers, who made sure everyone remained aboard through the storm. They weren't exempt from the storm, and the results weren't pretty: they eventually shipwrecked on an island, as Paul also said would happen. But God made provision. They placed all their confidence in the ship, their supplies, and their skills for their safety, but their skills were no match for the storm, and God took the supplies and the ship as well, leaving them with pieces. Still, they made it safely to shore, not by sailing on the ship but by clinging to pieces of the ship.

We don't always have the luxury of ships—of big houses, high-paying jobs, or good health. Our marriages aren't always perfect. Though we may lose our ships, God can still help us find His peace in the pieces we have left after the storm.

BEING HUMAN IS BEING BROKEN

If your life doesn't look like the complete picture of flourishing success you want, realize that to be human is to be broken. In other words, *brokenness is part of the human experience.*

In Genesis 2, Adam and Eve were whole and perfect individuals. Adam's hair, his teeth, his height, his limbs—everything was perfect. He was perfection, and so was Eve, just the way God made them. But one chapter later, they were eating from a forbidden tree (Genesis 3:6). Though God created man and woman in His image, their sin created a chasm in their relationship with Him. Hardship ensued because a life on earth without strife was no longer possible. Eve would have to suffer the pains of childbearing (Genesis 3:16), while Adam would have to work hard to survive (Genesis 3:17–19).

He would have to hustle, scrape, and scratch to feed himself and his family, because like Paul said to the Thessalonians, "The one who is unwilling to work shall not eat" (2 Thessalonians 3:10). Not everything is given or handed to us, because of sin.

Struggle and pain, challenge and heartache don't mean that you're a bad person. That's just how it is in this life because people since Adam and Eve have been imperfect, so this world and this life are imperfect. Paying your tithes and going to Sunday school won't change any of that. That's why Jesus told us in John 16:33 that we would have trouble, but He is greater than that trouble. Just like Paul and Job, we have God even when our lives are in pieces!

As we learned in previous chapters, our relationship with Christ doesn't inoculate us from storm, trials, and tribulations. Though Jesus can calm every storm, sometimes He wants to let a storm speak in our lives. God will let some storms rage for a while, like He let Satan have his way with Job's life for a time. But it's not a punishment. Your storm doesn't mean that your faith is deficient. It doesn't mean that you've done something bad in the eyes of God. If the disciples, Paul, and Jesus Himself suffered, why wouldn't you?

Not only is it inevitable, like Jesus said, but God also allows it, and He knows what He is doing in our lives. We can praise God when storms break our lives to pieces, as well as when we feel whole because life is treating us well. As Job said, "Naked I came from my mother's womb, and naked I will depart. The LORD gave and the LORD has taken away; may the name of the LORD be praised" (Job 1:21).

GOD USES BROKENNESS TO MAKE US WHOLE

It also glorifies God when we go through storms, which is why James said to "consider it pure joy" when we go through trials (James 1:2). *Being broken into pieces in a storm is one way God makes us more whole.* Like with the stained-glass art, pieces make up the whole.

If it were up to us, we'd never choose brokenness. I would never willingly go through any trial I've endured. But if I hadn't had those experiences, I wouldn't have the precious pieces of my life I have now. Our lives are the sum total of our experiences, including those that cause us pain and break us, leaving us in fragments and tatters. We are complete works of God, but our completeness doesn't mean our lives are woven of homogenous cloth. Our lives don't comprise one kind of experience or relationship. One victory, one defeat, one event, or one other person does not the whole of our lives make. Being human is being broken. Our brokenness leaves us in pieces, and our pieces make the whole.

With this truth in mind, if others try to equate you with one element or episode of your life—whether good or bad, mistake or success—don't accept that evaluation. You're much more complex than that. Don't try to walk out your journey based on others' simplistic, partial definitions of who you are. God created you in His likeness and for His glory. Therefore, He uses everything in your life to bring you to your destiny, making you who He wants you to be.

It is always interesting and sometimes amusing when people think they know me because of how they see me. People assume that a preacher loves nothing but Christian literature. They think a pastor would like nothing better as a gift than a cross or a statue of praying hands. All his birthday cards have Scripture in them. When people invite him to their house, he has to say grace, and everyone is at their holiest. But that's not all of who I am! I'm not just thirty-five minutes in a pulpit every Sunday. That's not all of my pieces or all of my story.

Our fragments and seasons are organized into a completed piece. We're mosaic art, like the "Crucifixion" piece, and mosaics, though potentially made of broken pieces of all kinds of materials and sources and colors, are beautiful when taken as a whole. We don't always know where exactly the pieces came from, and they may be shattered in all different ways, but the artist sees something greater than the fragments or their history. Likewise, God shapes our lives into beautiful works of art, according to His design.

So don't read too much into individual pieces of your life or anyone else's. The blood of Christ covers the ugly parts of our past and our hearts, the things broken by other people and circumstances and our own weakness, and makes us new and whole and beautiful, in His image.

Your Pieces Are Productive

In this way, *God makes your pieces productive*. The ship Paul was traveling on ran aground on a sandbar. Everyone except Paul might have set out thinking that the ship would carry them to their destination, but the storm overwhelmed it, leaving the Romans, the crew, and the prisoners fearful.

Storms that persist and upset the things in our lives that normally bring us a sense of security can leave us feeling scared, overwhelmed, and even abandoned by and doubtful of God. But storms don't get the last word, because the sovereign will of God is still at work. The will of God supersedes every other force. He may allow the storm to break up the entirety of your ship, but He will preserve the pieces of your life He wants preserved. God will use the pieces that remain to bring you ashore. He can get you where you need to go, producing necessary changes and growth in your life, using the broken pieces of a marriage, family, job, house, car, and bank account.

Don't fret or weep over the ship you lost. Cling to the pieces you have left, even if they're just your life and a word of Scripture and a song of praise, and keep calling on the name of the Lord. He specializes in broken pieces, so you can trust Him with yours. If you do, you'll have a peace that "transcends all understanding" (Philippians 4:7), even in the deadliest storm.

WORKBOOK

Chapter Six Questions

Question: What is your current internal (emotional and mental) state? How is it impacted by your external circumstances?

_____

_____

_____

_____

_____

_____

_____

_____

_____

Question: Is having God in your life enough for you? Does His presence sustain you and keep you at peace even when you feel like nothing is working out or like you have nothing else? Does this reveal any lack in your relationship with God?

_____

_____

_____

_____

_____

_____

_____

_____

Question: Are you comfortable with your brokenness, or do you feel like you will be content only if your life looks picture-perfect? How do you think God wants to use your brokenness in your life?

_____

_____

_____

_____

_____

_____

_____

_____

_____

Action: Search the Scriptures for verses to encourage you in seasons of loss. Then make a list of the things you feel you've lost in your life. Ask God to show you how He can use this loss and brokenness for Him. Read and meditate on the scriptures on your list until your sorrow over loss becomes hope for your future!

Chapter Six Notes

CHAPTER SEVEN

Trust God's Eye

When they arrived, Samuel saw Eliab and thought, "Surely the LORD's anointed stands here before the LORD."

But the LORD said to Samuel, "Do not consider his appearance or his height, for I have rejected him. The LORD does not look at the things people look at. People look at the outward appearance, but the LORD looks at the heart."

—*1 Samuel 16:6–7*

God has His ways for choosing the route we take and the storms we face on our journey, but how does He choose *us*? How does He evaluate people?

One of the biggest sporting events of the year doesn't involve any game or scoring of points. Instead of players wearing uniforms, broadcasters show up in suits and ties. Every spring, young players sit on the edge of their seats at home in front of the TV, waiting to be drafted into the National Football League. During the NFL draft, fans eagerly anticipate seeing which new players their favorite team will pick to bring on that year. Who will get the standout talent—the top college quarterback, running back, receiver, and so on—hangs in the balance.

One group of people critical to the draft process isn't made up of athletes and doesn't get the kind of fanfare the players or coaches do. NFL scouts are responsible for traveling the country before the draft, sitting in games and locker rooms, meeting with players' agents and team management, and even visiting players' homes to meet their families. These talent scouts have to understand the game and know what they're looking for. They're experts who have to evaluate size, speed, and athleticism as well as football acumen and decision-making ability. A scout looks at the whole profile of potential players to determine their value to NFL teams in the coming season. Is this player what the team needs to build the best, most competitive roster?

In the Old Testament, God used the prophet Samuel as a sort of scout to find the right candidate to be the new king of Israel because the current king, Saul, wasn't cutting it. Saul had gotten full of himself, prideful, and disobedient because he was concerned more with what people thought than what God thought, so God withdrew His anointing—His selection and favor—from Saul. In this case, unlike a team owner or manager, God already knew who the new king would be and where to find him. Samuel just had to do the legwork to identify this person.

In 1 Samuel 16, the prophet was sent to the home of Jesse in Bethlehem to anoint the next king of Israel. After Jesse and the town elders of Bethlehem joined Samuel for a sacrifice to

God, Samuel had a look at seven of Jesse's sons, all of whom had kingly traits based on man's superficiality. But God has His own way of evaluating and choosing people, and He does not make judgments the way people tend to do. God told Samuel that factors like appearance and height didn't matter, because "the LORD looks at the heart" (1 Samuel 16:7).

When God was choosing the future king of Israel, these seven sons of Jesse didn't make the cut. He wanted "a man after his own heart" (1 Samuel 13:14). Then Samuel told Jesse to bring his youngest son, David. In the eyes of his father and others, David was only a humble shepherd, not even worth mentioning up front, but in God's eye, David was the only person fit to be king of His people. And so, through His prophet, God selected David, whom we know as one of the most prominent figures in all of Scripture, to succeed Saul as the king of Israel.

This scriptural episode gives us insight into how God chooses each of us. We all want to be chosen and used by God to accomplish great things, and He does have purposes for us all. Some of us may already be walking in His purposes for us, at least in part. Regardless, we must understand that God has a particular way of evaluating and choosing us, which is different from human ways. When people ascribe value to themselves or someone else, we tend to do it by comparing each other. Human methods of evaluation are superficial, shallow.

God, however, knows what He is looking for. He has an eye for what man cannot see, and these things—the things in our hearts—are what He values when He picks someone for a purpose.

GOD HAS ALREADY CHOSEN YOU

Note that God's choice had already been made from the outset. When He sent Samuel to Jesse in Bethlehem, He said, "I have chosen one of his sons to be king" (1 Samuel 16:1). What's more, long before Jesse knew that he would have sons or what their names would be, God had chosen David to be king.

If you're waiting on God to pick you, realize that *He has already made a decision*. Before you were born, He knew where He wanted to place you and for what purpose. Though God allows us to make our own decisions, His plans don't depend on our choices or actions. God's sovereign will shall always come to pass. He always does what He wants, when He wants to do it, for whatever reasons please Him.

The next time you're wrestling in your mind with how and when your situation will come together or work itself out, consider that God has already figured it out. Before trouble started looking in your direction, God made a decision about whether to allow it, for how long, and for what purposes. He made His decisions about you before anyone else decided whether you were strong, fast, good-looking, healthy, wealthy, or smart enough.

So just keep living your life, being faithful to God, and studying His Word. Keep trusting Him and pressing forward. Day after day, keep praising and praying to Him. It won't change God's mind, so you can rest in the fact that He has already made all His decisions about you and your life. Nothing can frustrate the choices God makes.

GOD CHOOSES FROM WHAT ONLY HE SEES

Jesse surely felt flattered that one of his sons was going to be king, at the center of a new thing God was about to do with Israel. Maybe he was boasting about his older sons and their accomplishments. When Eliab walked in—tall, dark, and handsome—we might imagine that he looked like the very specimen of human perfection. Whatever "it" is, from physical strength to a kingly walk, he seemed to have it, because even God's prophet assumed this was surely the guy. *"This has to be the Lord's anointed,"* he thought excitedly.

But God told the prophet explicitly that Eliab wasn't the one and explained that He looks at the inside, not the outside. God judges by the things only He can see. *God chooses from the inside.*

This tells us that we don't need to concern ourselves so much with measuring up in the ways other people can see. You may not be as smart, as experienced, or as pretty or handsome as the people in line next to you. Your background may not be as impressive as that of the other candidates for the job. But those factors don't carry weight with God the way they do with people. People consider superficial matters, but only God knows His criteria for the task He has in mind.

Some assignments He hands out may require a short person, a plain person, a person who didn't go to college, or a person who came from the wrong side of the tracks. There is no use trying to tailor your résumé for God's anointing for a certain purpose, because the very things you think He wants might be the very things He is rejecting. What we do know is that God judges from the inside out. While so many of us waste our efforts trying to make our outside look as good as or better than someone else's, God sees right through us. The only résumé He examines is the heart.

In football, some players may not be as fast or as tall as others or have the most impressive stats, but they have something special on the inside that makes them stand out. In a recent season of the reality show *Hard Knocks*, a behind-the-scenes look at NFL teams and players, Dallas Cowboys owner Jerry Jones talked about star quarterback Dakota Prescott.[9] Though the Cowboys first picked him up in the second half (fourth round) of the 2016 draft, without any fanfare, they knew as soon as Dak Prescott walked into the Cowboys' training facility that he was something special. It had nothing to do with his physicality. When he talked to people, they couldn't help but like him. He had an unquantifiable charisma.

God looks for unquantifiable value in us. You may not think you're as impressive on the surface as the next person, but you have what God put inside you and who He made you to be. He put something special in David and told Samuel that was what mattered.

God put something in each of us, and He will use each of us mightily for His purposes. You don't have to be everyone's preference; you only need to keep being who God designed you to be, on the inside and the outside. You don't have to attract other people's notice, only God's. He will make sure that the right people see you at the right time.

I've been called arrogant and stuck-up, weak, slow, too loud, or too quiet. It used to get to me, but now I accept that I don't have to do things the way any other person wants me to. I only need to do it the way God intended when He made me.

YOUR START DOESN'T DETERMINE YOUR FINISH

In the 2000 NFL draft, the 199th pick out of 254 was a quarterback named Tom Brady.[10] Though he entered the NFL in the most unremarkable way, starting near the bottom, over the next two decades, he led the New England Patriots to six Super Bowl wins and won a seventh Super Bowl with the Tampa Bay Buccaneers.

Clearly, *your origination does not determine your destination.* How you start does not determine how you finish—thank God! Don't let humble beginnings speak over how you finish.

Jesse figured that David was beneath Samuel's interest. Unlike some of his brothers, he wasn't yet a soldier or someone women admired. He didn't have their height or breadth of shoulder. Worst of all, he smelled like sheep. As far as Jesse was concerned, he had only seven sons in the running to be the future king of Israel. But God already had His eye on

Jesse's eighth son, and He always had.

Maybe you smell like sheep today, but you could be wearing a crown tomorrow. There are no insignificant roles in God's economy, and He uses every season as training for what comes next in your life. All of your sheep-tending now will pay off in God's timing. Be faithful in your sheep-tending, because God put something special in you, and He knows where to find you when the time is right.

If you're worried about your background or your pedigree, remember that a shepherd with the right heart is the perfect candidate to rule a kingdom. Jesus Himself was born to a carpenter and a teenaged mother in a manger used to feed animals, and now we know Him as the King of kings and Lord of lords.

The world has its standards for what it deems worthy: our appearance, our degrees, our car, our zip code. Man looks on the outside, but God looks at the heart. He doesn't care where you came from or who your mother and father were. He cares that He made you in His image. Trust that God has His own way of evaluating and choosing. His eye sees the king or queen in you the world cannot see.

WORKBOOK

Chapter Seven Questions

Question: Do you trust that God has your life figured out, or do you think it's up to you to work things out? Do you find it difficult to follow God's leading when it contradicts *your* plan? Why or why not?

_____

_____

_____

_____

_____

_____

_____

_____

_____

Question: Are you more focused on becoming what this world wants or on becoming who God created you to be? In what ways do the expectations of culture and society hinder you from being faithful to God's leading in your life?

_____

_____

_____

_____

_____

_____

_____

_____

_____

_____

Question: What is the state of your heart? Are you more focused on outward accomplishments or on inward transformations? What area of your heart, if any, do you still need to surrender to God?

_____

_____

_____

_____

_____

_____

_____

_____

_____

_____

_____

Action: On a sheet of paper, create three columns. At the top of the first column, write "Five Years Ago." Label the second column, "Right Now," and the third column, "Five Years from Now."

In the column labeled "Five Years Ago," write whatever comes to mind about where you were in life five years in the past, including the kind of person you were, your perspective, how you made decisions, etc. Then, in the column labeled "Right Now," describe yourself and your life currently, including similar kinds of details. Do you notice any differences and changes?

Now, in the final column ("Five Years from Now"), write whatever comes to mind about where you want to be in life, the kind of person you hope to be, the perspective you want to grow into, the way you want to make decisions, etc., as you continue on your journey.

Chapter Seven Notes

CHAPTER EIGHT

Grace Over Stones

...but Jesus went to the Mount of Olives.

At dawn he appeared again in the temple courts, where all the people gathered around him, and he sat down to teach them. The teachers of the law and the Pharisees brought in a woman caught in adultery. They made her stand before the group and said to Jesus, "Teacher, this woman was caught in the act of adultery. In the Law Moses commanded us to stone such women. Now what do you say?" They were using this question as a trap, in order to have a basis for accusing him.

But Jesus bent down and started to write on the ground with his finger. When they kept on questioning him, he straightened up and said to them, "Let any one of you who is without sin be the first to throw a stone at her." Again he stooped down and wrote on the ground.

At this, those who heard began to go away one at a time, the older ones first, until only Jesus was left, with the woman still standing there. Jesus straightened up and asked her, "Woman, where are they? Has no one condemned you?"

"No one, sir," she said.

God Has a Way

> *"Then neither do I condemn you," Jesus declared. "Go now and leave your life of sin."*
>
> —*John 8:1–11*

On July 12, 1997, a girl named Malala was born in the Swat Valley of Pakistan to father Ziauddin Youesfzai and mother Tor Pekai Youesfzai.[11] Though, culturally, to raise a daughter in Pakistan was considered more of a burden than a joy, Ziauddin loved his daughter so much that he became the teacher of a girl's school in their home city of Mingora. Young Malala embraced her early years of education.

Then, between 2007 and 2008, the Taliban took control of the region and invoked harsh measures. Among other things, the Taliban prohibited girls from going to school. Eleven-year-old Malala couldn't continue to receive the education that mattered so much to her and her father.

But the Taliban didn't count on Malala's resolve. She began to speak out, expressing her disdain for the rule of the Taliban. She brought attention to the injustice of Pakistani girls being unable to advance or improve their lives through education, even in the twenty-first century.

Eventually, the Taliban began to target her, and in 2012, Taliban members ambushed her on a bus while she was riding home from school. Though critically injured, with extensive medical care in the U.K., she survived—and she would not be silenced.

She started the Malala Fund to raise awareness and money for the education of other girls like her in the face of oppression so they would have the opportunity to learn and grow on par with boys. In 2014, she became the youngest-ever Nobel laureate, winning the Nobel Peace Prize. The Taliban could not snuff her out, and their attempts to do so had backfired spectacularly.

In an episode in the Gospel of John, the Pharisees also targeted a woman, using her as a pawn to try to trap Jesus in contradicting the law of Moses. A woman had been caught in adultery, and there was a mob ready to ensure that she suffered consequences to the fullest extent of the law: stoning. They invited Jesus to weigh in on her deserved punishment.

Now, we might raise questions: How did they come to catch this woman in an act of adultery? What exactly did they mean by "such women"? But Jesus masterfully avoided their trap, indirectly pushing back on the misguided premises and deceitful motivation of their question to Him and their judgment of the woman. Instead of answering the Pharisees immediately, He knelt and wrote something—we don't know what—in the dirt (John 8:6). Then He told them that any of them who were "without sin" should begin carrying out the punishment they said she deserved under the law.

We can imagine the sound of the mob's stones dropping to the ground, one by one, as they realized that Jesus had turned the trap around on them. They couldn't follow through with their judgment against this woman without claiming that there was no sin in their own lives, which everyone knew would be a lie. The crowd dissipated, leaving only Jesus and the woman. Since Jesus wouldn't condemn her to stoning and no one else remained, she was free.

Of course, Jesus didn't free her to commit more adultery.

He freed her to leave her old, sinful way of life behind. The grace of God made this possible because His grace was more than a match for the stones of judgment. In our lives, too, God has a way of balancing rebuke and restoration. While we deserve the stones, God chooses to deal with us in grace. By doing this, He takes our messes, our sin, and turns the situation around to His glory while still holding us accountable.

WE ALL DESERVE STONES

In His way, God keeps us all in check, the sinners and the accusers. Each of us can identify with both parties in this story. We have been the woman caught in our sin, and we have been the Pharisees disgusted by someone else's sin. Thanks be to God for His unmerited favor and grace!

I say "unmerited" because *we all deserve stones*. If you think that because you've been saved and know Jesus and read your Bible, you don't commit sins deserving condemnation, I have to burst your bubble. Being on the church board or going to seminary doesn't change this, either. None of us is perfect, and we all have stuff we're not proud of. We're glad that other people don't know about some of it, but we can't hide any part of our sinful mess from God. "All have sinned and fall short of the glory of God," Paul's letter to the Romans tells us (Romans 3:23). So, who do we think we are to walk through this world as if we're wearing halos? We're all sinners, and any claim to the contrary is a lie from the pit of hell.

Notice that in the story, the woman didn't deny that she

was a sinner. She didn't try to defend herself, and she didn't name names, even though you can't commit adultery by yourself. According to the Levitical law, death by stoning was the penalty for adultery. But the Pharisees weren't really concerned about upholding the law in this situation, or else they would have tried to bring all guilty parties, men included, to judgment. Their appeals to the law of Moses were hypocritical because they targeted only the woman and their motive was to put Jesus in an awkward position.

Even our salvation doesn't excuse us or make us immune to sin, which also means we should never get excited about exposing someone else's sin. None of us has received "catching other people in sin so we can go tell someone else" as a personal ministry from God. If you think otherwise, that's your own sinful, hypocritical nature at work, not Jesus. Stop getting on the phone and gossiping about who's doing what with whom! And stop feeding someone doing that by asking for more information.

You can claim as often and loudly as you want that being saved makes you bulletproof to sin, but Satan will trip you up and make a liar of you soon enough. The enemy knows you better than you know yourself, including your weaknesses. He knows what you like even when you're not supposed to have it.

Salvation doesn't remove all your past sin, either. You still did all of those sinful things back in the day. Your faith and repentance may separate you from the eternal consequences of your sin "as far as the east is from the west" (Psalm 103:12), but you still committed the sin. If your trust is in what Jesus accomplished on the cross, He won't hold your sin against you, but don't pretend that you didn't do it.

CONDEMNATION CUTS BOTH WAYS

We all deserve stones, as Jesus reminded the Pharisees and the mob, and this also means *condemnation for sin cuts two ways*. The Pharisees made it their business to expose the woman's sin, laying out her dirty laundry for everyone to see. They didn't care about her or her sin, but about using her to condemn Jesus as a fraud. Yet by condemning her, they would be condemning themselves as well.

There is no honor in exposing the sin of another person. Beware of people who know all the best gossip about everyone else but never volunteer any information about their own sin and weakness. There is plenty of fodder for gossip about them, too, only they want to pretend otherwise. Accusations against others serve to deflect attention from their own guilt. Gossip is a way of preying on other people to make themselves feel strong. It's even worse when it's done in the name of the kingdom of God by someone claiming, "I just want to help you in your sin and get some other people involved." All of this serves the accuser's self-righteousness and weakness, not your well-being.

It takes an unhappy person to want to rub someone else's face in the dirt. By contrast, I will be the first to tell you that I fall short of God's glory. I am a sinner saved only by the grace of God. I've done many things I'm not proud of, but I'm covered by the blood of Jesus Christ. Paul wrote in

Romans 6:23 that "the gift of God is eternal life in Christ Jesus our Lord."

Talking about my sins and shortcomings won't put me in hell or in heaven. Other people can shame me, but God will continue to bless me. I still feel the dawning of every new day and sing praises to His name because Jesus answers my accusers, "If you have no sin, you can throw the first stone." And they all have to drop their stones.

It wasn't only that the people in the crowd dropped their stones because they recognized their own sinfulness. They also knew, like Jesus knew, that the Levitical law said only the witnesses to the crime were allowed to cast the stones. Had any of the Pharisees actually witnessed the woman committing adultery? And if so, were they merely witnesses or also somehow participants in the alleged sinful acts? We don't know all the details, but I wouldn't be surprised if Jesus stooped in the sand to write the names of men in the crowd who were just as guilty as the woman.

We aren't responsible for condemning others. Stop thinking it's your job to tell others how wrong they are and what their punishment ought to be. Scripture tells us that if our brother is caught in sin, we are to restore him gently (Galatians 6:1), but we tend to emphasize the catching over the restoration. Thank God that Jesus is in the business of restoring us! Womanizers, prostitutes, felons, liars, people who left their spouse, and people who had children out of wedlock can all be blessed and used by God. Our sin doesn't define us, but that's only because God's grace outweighs the stones we deserve. So let's talk less about our individual sins and more about our God, whose grace covers our sins.

The Pharisees' desire to condemn the woman revealed the darkness in their own hearts. Be careful how you speak about other people. Take pause before you speak disparagingly of someone else, because God knows that your sins are just as filthy as theirs. You may have everyone else fooled, but God was right there, witnessing your sin every step of the way. Jesus preached in the Sermon on the Mount, "Do not judge, or you too will be judged" (Matthew 7:1). No one else had the right to cast stones on the woman except Jesus, and He had the right to cast stones on her accusers, too.

How dare we point out "the speck of sawdust" in someone else's eye when we have two-by-fours in our own eyes (Matthew 7:3)? How dare we make someone else's public downfall our business when we have no intention of helping that person? Our hypocritical tendency is to use other people's downfall as leverage to lift ourselves up in our own estimation and others'. It gives us comfort in our own spiritual squalor.

Too often, people in the church like to pounce on transgendered and homosexual people. Words like "abomination" and "sin" get thrown around all too readily. These people may be told that they are condemned to hell and aren't welcome in the body of Christ. But who are we to deny a person caught in sin access to the grace of God? The rest of us must resist the temptation to consider ourselves worthier than others of His grace. Maybe the only difference is that some of us live our sin in the dark because we know it's sin, while others live their sin transparently, with an authenticity

I think some professing Christians secretly envy, because those people haven't had the undeserved blessing of knowing Jesus.

If you want to condemn someone else, you'd better make sure you're never promiscuous, proud, deceitful, or envious. I can hear stones dropping to the ground right now.

GRACE OVERRIDES THE RULES

Fortunately for all of us, *grace overrides the rules*. For each of us who has committed sin, the rules are clear: the penalty is death. The Pharisees weren't wrong about the prescribed penalty for the woman who committed adultery. But grace, in the person of Jesus, had something else to say. The rules say that the woman should have died, as should we, but Jesus refused to condemn her, as He refuses to condemn us who believe in Him for salvation.

The woman's guilt didn't disqualify her from God's grace. We're all guilty, and we've all fallen. But by the grace of God—not our education, our insurance, or our bank account—we escape punishment. Friends in high places can't save you from death; only the highest of friends in the highest of places, the Lord of lords, Jesus in heaven, can accomplish that. The Pharisees who thought they were dragging the woman to judgment and death were, in fact, carrying her to grace and new life at the feet of Jesus. The rules called for stones, but grace called for freedom.

It's unfortunate that there was more zeal over the adulterous woman's judgment and punishment than there was over the condition of her soul. She needed accountability, but she was still valuable and worthy of love. Jesus' words both held her accountable and affirmed her value. His words also show us that we're not in a position to judge. The Pharisees' judgment only pushed this woman to Jesus, where she experienced His grace.

I remind you again that, as Paul wrote in Romans 3:23, no one avoids sin completely and we all "fall short of the glory of God." Yet, even though we all are guilty and justice demands our death, we do not stand condemned in the eyes of God, because Jesus has paid the price for us. His blood satisfies the demands of God's justice so that, in Jesus, we find infinite grace that covers a multitude of sins.

We are only here, in our present state of salvation and relationship with God, by His grace. We walk through our day by the grace of God, who cleaned us up, turned us around, and put our feet on solid ground at the foot of the cross. Only He could accomplish this, through Jesus. We ought to inhale His grace and exhale His praises in worship! It's His grace that allows us new possibilities and opportunities every morning of our journey.

WORKBOOK

Chapter Eight Questions

Question: Do you relate more to the accuser or the accused (John 8:1–11)? How does your answer reflect that you are in need of Jesus? In what ways can you pursue a greater balance of grace and accountability in your life?

_____

_____

_____

_____

_____

_____

_____

_____

_____

_____

_____
_____

Question: Have you ever used concern for another person as an excuse to engage in gossip or perpetuate judgment, exposing someone else's weaknesses while elevating yourself? Has anyone ever done that to you? What would be a better way to handle situations like that moving forward?

_____
_____
_____
_____
_____
_____
_____
_____
_____
_____

Question: Is it difficult for you to accept God's grace? Do you ever feel that you need to get your behavior in check before God can extend His love and grace to you? What does the Bible say about God's grace?

_____
_____
_____
_____
_____
_____
_____
_____
_____

Action: Have you been judging anyone in your life instead of extending grace? What are some things you can do in the coming days, weeks, or months to extend God's grace to that person?

Do you need to accept God's grace for something in your own life? Spend some time confessing to God and allowing Him to extend His grace to you.

Chapter Eight Notes

CHAPTER NINE

The Truth About Failure

"Don't be alarmed," he said. "You are looking for Jesus the Nazarene, who was crucified. He has risen! He is not here. See the place where they laid him. But go, tell his disciples and Peter, 'He is going ahead of you into Galilee. There you will see him, just as he told you.'"

—**Mark 16:6–7**

Mark 16 describes how three women brought spices to Jesus' tomb to anoint His body. They weren't sure how they were going to roll away the large stone from the tomb, but when they arrived, they saw it had already been rolled away. To their astonishment, a young man wearing a white robe was sitting inside, but he told them not to be frightened by the fact that Jesus' body was missing. Miraculously, Jesus was alive and was already heading for Galilee to meet the disciples. Specifically, the young man, an angel, told these women to relay his message to Peter.

This is remarkable because Peter had failed Jesus. He had

failed as a disciple of Jesus, claiming not even to know Him, yet Jesus had a way to restore Peter to a relationship with Him. This is encouraging to us because we all fail, too, yet God has made a way for our comeback.

Everyone appreciates a good comeback story because we identify with the underdog, the one who is cast aside and counted out. In Chapter Two, we learned about Joseph's comeback story from slavery and prison to prime minister. From movie characters like Maximus in *Gladiator*, who rises from exile to defy a treacherous emperor,[12] to sports figures like golfer Tiger Woods, who won a Masters tournament in 2019 after more than a decade without a major championship win,[13] comeback stories encourage us in our seasons of trial. Comebacks remind us that anything is possible, even victory out of the least-promising circumstances.

Jesus' death on the cross and resurrection, the pinnacle of the Christian story, is the ultimate comeback story. It's the main event in the history of the world and the whole order created by God. Nothing else is as grand or spectacular as the resurrected Savior!

For thirty years, Jesus grew up in humble circumstances. His family lived in a place called Nazareth, a place the rich and powerful thought was worthless. Then, for the last three years of His life on earth, He walked among the people, from place to place, mending broken bodies and healing broken souls. He even raised the dead back to life.

In the end, one of His closest followers betrayed Him, selling Him out to His enemies, who beat, bruised, and battered Him. In court, He was railroaded, convicted, and sentenced to death. He died on a cross and was buried in a grave one of His followers donated. This is a comeback story because He didn't stay there.

Before His death on a cross, Jesus predicted that His disciple Peter would deny Him three times (Matthew 26:34), but Peter insisted this would never happen (Matthew 26:35). However, as Peter waited outside the high priest's house after Jesus' arrest to find out what would happen, other people confronted him about being a follower of Jesus. Frightened by what they might do to him, Peter denied it—three times. He had failed to keep his promise: "Even if all fall away on account of you, I never will" (Matthew 26:33).

Your journey to becoming the person God planned for you to be is not along a straight road. It spirals through seasons of heartache and pain as well as victory. There will be failure, but the angel's specific mention of Peter in his message to the women and the disciples should inform your perspective on failure. If you find yourself beaten up by failures or other people keep throwing your mistakes in your face, take note that God has something more to say about the times you've fallen short.

No One Is Perfect

Failing is as fundamental to living as breathing. *Failure is an integral part of the human condition.* It's often said but still profoundly true that no one is perfect. Though the Trinity made us in the likeness of God, humankind has been fallen since Adam and Eve, as we saw in Chapter Six. In fact, everyone has it in him or her to fail, and everyone has failed, no exceptions. Stay away from anyone who claims otherwise, because they're failing in the very act of telling you as much. Whether intentionally deceitful or unwittingly prideful, they are speaking a lie. Everyone misses the mark sometimes, which should bring us comfort in our errors.

We can mess up but keep on because God preserves us for His purposes. He didn't discount Peter, who denied Him, and He won't discount us. We just have to repent, continue trusting Him, and accept His grace.

You Benefit from Your Failures

Not only is failure normal and inevitable in our lives, but *it is also beneficial.* We find our failures embarrassing, especially when other people remind us of them constantly and use them to shame us. Failure isn't good, of course, yet God teaches us lessons in our failures as surely as you learn a painful but valuable lesson the first time you touch a hot stove. Failure humbles us when we need to be knocked down a peg. It gives us a contrite heart so we can understand and remember our need for Jesus.

In a 1997 commercial, basketball legend Michael Jordan described failure as a part of eventual success: "I've missed more than nine thousand shots in my career. I've lost almost three hundred games. ... I've failed over and over and over again in my life. And that is why I succeed." Those missed shots and lost games were necessary to the points Jordan scored and the games he helped his team win.[14]

Failure isn't the opposite of success; it's part of success. It's our teacher, not our undertaker. The true opposite of success, the only failure that would stick, is giving up or not even trying. This isn't to say that we should fail on purpose. But when we genuinely try and still fall short, God has a way of helping us learn from our failures.

Maybe you can find inspiration in the phoenix, the mythical bird that was said to burst periodically into flame and be reborn from the ashes. The phoenix had to burn to be reborn and make its comeback.

Your Failures Don't Diminish God

After Peter denied Jesus three times and remembered Jesus' prediction that this would happen, "he broke down and wept" (Mark 14:72). Peter's failure certainly affected Peter, but it did not diminish Jesus in the slightest. *Our failure does not lessen God or take away from His glory.*

This disciple who had proclaimed his unbreakable devotion and love toward Jesus had revealed the weakness and darkness lurking in his heart. When servant girls and others in the priest's courtyard had identified Peter as one of Jesus' followers, Peter had tried to shut it down. He'd said they were speaking nonsense (Mark 14:68), and he'd even cursed them out (Mark 14:71). Like so many of us, when Peter was called out, he got defensive, and things got ugly. Fear for his life had overwhelmed his love for his Lord when the situation got real.

Belatedly, realization of his failure overwhelmed him, and

the tears of contrition flowed. Preserving his life from Jesus' enemies hadn't spared him from failure. Likewise, you might lie to everyone else and fool everyone else, functioning at a high level and appearing to be the epitome of success, yet you and God will still know that you've failed. We carry some of our deepest, darkest secrets to the grave, even as others may celebrate our success.

But Peter's failure didn't diminish Jesus' glory. It didn't disrupt God's redemptive plan that He had set in motion before the creation of the world (1 Peter 1:20). God's plan rolled right along. In fact, Peter's dismal failure didn't even diminish Jesus' plan to use Peter to spread the gospel, work miracles, and save souls in Jesus' name. After all, He had known from the beginning, when He first called Peter to drop his fishing nets and follow Him (Matthew 4:19), that Peter would deny Him one day.

But God still had a way for Peter, as He always had! His message to the women for the disciples even specified "and Peter," calling him alone by name. He didn't call Matthew, Thomas, Andrew, James, John, or any of the others, regardless of whether or not they had been more faithful to Jesus than Peter had been. Though Peter had fallen, he could still be redeemed.

In other words, failure is not fatal. Your failures cannot disrupt the redemptive work of Jesus in your life or anyone else's. No matter how far you've fallen, He is not surprised, and He still has a way to use you. There is still room for you at the cross, and His deliverance is just as powerful as it was before you messed up.

No one escapes failure, but failure does not have to be final. In Christ, there is a place to return to even after the worst of failures. No matter how bad we've failed, no matter our poor judgment and our moments of frailty, we can come back. When we walk outside of the lines God has drawn for us, there is a Savior who knows our name. Instead of giving us the rundown of all our sins and failures, He is ready to call us back into a life of relationship and service.

WORKBOOK

Chapter Nine Questions

Question: Describe a time when you failed at something or failed God. How did that impact your relationship with God?

_____
_____
_____
_____
_____
_____
_____
_____
_____
_____

Question: What is your comeback story? If you feel you don't have one yet, what do you hope it will be?

_____
_____
_____
_____
_____
_____
_____
_____
_____

Question: Is there anything in your life—a failure, a mistake, or a struggle—that you need to come back from right now? How do you think God wants you to approach that failure, and what steps can you take to be restored in Christ?

_____
_____
_____
_____
_____

_____

_____

_____

_____

_____

_____

Action: Find or draw a picture of a phoenix. Write or type a verse on it that reminds you of God's grace and fills you with hope for your own comeback when you experience failure. Either frame and hang it or place it somewhere you can refer to it when you find yourself in need of encouragement.

Chapter Nine Notes

CHAPTER TEN

How God Makes Good

And we know that in all things God works for the good of those who love him, who have been called according to his purpose.
—***Romans 8:28***

Perhaps no passage of Scripture is quoted more during tough times than Romans 8:28, and in this book, we've already discovered how it encourages us when God sends us down a long, difficult route to our destination. Paul's words to the Romans remind us that God will strengthen us throughout our journey and use our hardship for good.

"Good" may seem an elusive, abstract term when the news is filled with mass shootings, police shootings, natural disasters, wars, inflation, and pandemics, yet the word of God says that everything works together for our good. We may read this promise and want to push back; I understand the impulse because sometimes so do I. When we receive bad news about our job, our health, or our loved ones, we want to talk back to God, asking how it could possibly be for our good or anyone else's. Where is the positive in the adverse situations we face?

In reading Romans 8:28, it seems we tend to put our emphasis in the wrong place, focusing more on "good" than on "God." When we read that "all things work together," we're comparing those words with the word "good." Our instinct is also to predetermine what "good" means. We want to qualify, quantify, and otherwise define it in a way that makes the most sense to us.

Therein lies the problem, because our definition of "good" is based on our limited perspective. What we call "good" may not be what God calls "good." What God wants to do in our lives may not line up with what we recognize as good, especially in the moment. Therefore, it's easy for us to miss the good things God is doing.

We'd be better served focusing on "God," the subject, instead of on our limited human notion of "good." God is the one who makes good, knitting it together in the way only He can. He is the one above everything. He knows everything and is everywhere. Though we find ourselves troubled because we don't see the good in the world or in our circumstances, let's stop looking for good and look for God instead.

ALL THINGS WORK TOGETHER FOR YOUR GOOD

When God makes good, He does it in His own way and uses everything. *All* things work together for our good. This includes the sunshine and the rain, wind, thunder, and lightning.

In the early days of the COVID-19 pandemic, my family and I were sheltering in place in our home and trying to find ways to occupy ourselves. One activity we took up was putting together puzzles. The highlight of the week was opening up a new puzzle on the dining room table. Initially, when the pieces fell out of the box, there was no organization. Some pieces didn't even look like they belonged in the puzzle. It didn't always make sense, but we trusted that all the pieces would fit together and eventually look like the picture on the box.

More than once, we'd get frustrated, thinking that surely some pieces were missing. Things didn't look right to us; pieces didn't seem to fit correctly. Then we'd realize we were trying to force pieces into places they didn't belong.

God works constantly in our lives, and He knows where all the pieces fit. You may think that things aren't working in your life, but God knows what He is doing as He incorporates painful circumstances like unemployment, disease, and divorce into the puzzle of your life, according to His design.

Next time you're questioning God, wondering how your negative circumstances could possibly be working together for good, remember that *all* means *all*. It's not your job to design the puzzle, create the pieces, or decide where they go. If that were the case, you wouldn't be trusting God with your life. We praise God because we can't fix what is broken, but He can. When we get frustrated, we take comfort and rest in praising Him because He makes good where we're incapable.

In His transcendence, God is totally independent of the created order. Therefore, He can make sweetness out of trouble and masterpieces out of messes.

GOD WORKS ALL THINGS *TOGETHER*

Paul also made clear in this scripture that God works all of these things *together*. The good-feeling stuff and the bad-feeling stuff, the sweet and the salty, complement each other in your life. Bold and beautiful come together with broken and busted in God's design for your journey. Every episode in your life is productive.

Some versions of the Bible translate Romans 8:28 as saying that "all things work together for good" (NKJV) so that "all things" is the grammatical subject, whereas the New International Version makes God the subject, who works in all things. In this respect, I think the NIV conveys the more accurate sense of the scripture, because if your circumstances are what's working in your life, God is not God. Who is controlling the storm? Who controls the darkness? God does. Without God working behind the scenes in your situation, you would be without hope.

God is in control of all the elements in your situation,

including the difficult and painful ones, weaving them together with every other thing to produce good in your life. He is the master baker, infinitely creative, and all your circumstances are ingredients in His recipe for your life. Nothing in your life is useless.

GOD ALWAYS HAS YOUR DESTINATION IN SIGHT

God sees your destination clearly; His eye is always fixed on His purposes. Because we tend to view our lives one episode at a time, we see only what's evident in the moment: when there's sickness, we see sickness. But God sees sickness *and* victory at the same time. *He always has the end in sight* when He makes good.

God sees your whole life at a glance, and what He sees is good. Though it doesn't always *feel* good, it's always *for* your good if you're called by Him—if you know Him, love Him, and have a relationship with Him. Trust God, confessing His name and accepting Him in your heart, and He will make nothing but good in your life. His perfect plan for you offers you "hope and a future" (Jeremiah 29:11), all of it beneficial for you. If it didn't happen the way He planned, according to His recipe, you'd miss something. Some element of the flavor or texture would be off if you didn't go through this trial or that heartache. Trust the master baker!

Tony Evans wrote that one time he was on a flight from Raleigh, North Carolina, back to Fort Worth. When the plane was about to land, the pilot announced that a storm had settled over the Dallas–Fort Worth area, so they'd have to divert to Abilene, Texas. When the plane landed there, one of the passengers told a flight attendant that Abilene was actually their final destination; they'd been headed to Forth Worth for a connecting flight. This passenger wanted to get off the plane because they were already home. Sometimes when God allows turbulence to divert us unexpectedly, the new route ends up being our intended destination.[15]

We can't help but struggle with seeing good come out of turbulence, especially our painful experiences. We believe we have a healthy understanding of what is good, but because we are of flesh and created by God, we will never be totally on par with God in our understanding of good. That is the primary reason why God is the one who uses all to make good. He makes all of life's experiences complement each other and work cooperatively in order for good to come to pass in the lives of those whom He has called.

God uses all the circumstances in our lives—the good, the bad, and the ugly—to bring about the good He desires. So stop worrying about the good and concern yourself instead with God, who knows what's really good. God is at work in every circumstance, ensuring that all things work out for our benefit, no matter how ugly they are.

We've seen throughout this book that God has unique ways to comfort, care for, and watch over us. His ways can seem peculiar to us, to say the least! As we read in Isaiah 55:8, God's thoughts and ways are different from ours. Sometimes He chooses the long way or the difficult way for us. We must trust that the course we're on is of divine design. God has His own reasons for setting the course the way He does, but good is always His endgame, and He has a way of making it happen.

WORKBOOK

Chapter Ten Questions

Question: What do you think God means when He promises to use all things for *good*? How might His definition of *good* be different from yours?

_____
_____
_____
_____
_____
_____
_____
_____
_____
_____

Question: Are you more focused on your circumstances and how they feel to you than on God and your relationship with Him? How can a focus on your current situation and its apparent trajectory hinder your connection to God?

_____

_____

_____

_____

_____

_____

_____

_____

_____

Question: What impact do you think focusing on your relationship with God will have on your circumstances or your perspective on life? What changes can you make to begin reorienting your focus?

_____

_____

_____

_____

_____

_____

_____

_____

_____

_____

_____

Action: Choose a story in the Bible about something challenging, painful, or unpleasant that happened. Then write a description of all the ways you can see that God used that situation for good in the lives of those involved or for the good of the whole world.

Chapter Ten Notes

About the Author

Howard is a native of Fort Worth, Texas, and has resided in Grand Rapids, Michigan, since 2005. He holds degrees from the University of Houston, Southwestern Baptist Theological Seminary, and Western Theological Seminary. Alongside pastoral service in the city of Grand Rapids, he has served on several boards and committees working to improve quality of life for underserved groups and communities in Kent County. Of all that he has experienced and accomplished, his greatest honor and privilege is to be husband to his wife, K'Sandra, and father to their three children, Zachary, Dylan Camille, and Natalie.

About Renown Publishing

Renown Publishing was founded with one mission in mind: to make your great idea famous.

At Renown Publishing, we don't just publish. We work hard to pair strategy with innovative marketing techniques so that your book launch is the start of something bigger.

Learn more at RenownPublishing.com.

REFERENCES

Notes

1. "Global Positioning System History." National Aeronautics and Space Administration. October 27, 2012. https://www.nasa.gov/directorates/heo/scan/communications/policy/GPS_History.html.

2. Merriam-Webster.com Dictionary, "sovereign." https://www.merriam-webster.com/dictionary/sovereign.

3. Tinley, Charles Albert. "We'll Understand It Better By and By." 1905.

4. PBS and GBH Educational Foundation. "Lightning Produces Nitrates." https://mpt.pbslearningmedia.org/resource/nves.sci.earth.nitrate/lightning-produces-nitrates/.

5. Britannica, "Hurricane Katrina." https://www.britannica.com/event/Hurricane-Katrina.

6. Belles, Jonathan. "5 Things Hurricanes Can Do That Are Actually Good." The Weather Channel. August 29, 2017. https://weather.com/storms/hurricane/news/hurricane-landfall-benefits-2016.

7. Focus on the Family. "Sea of Galilee Geography." That the World May Know with Ray Vander Laan. https://www.thattheworldmayknow.com/sea-of-galilee-geography.

8. McVicar, Brian. "ArtPrize 2011 Winner, 'Crucifixion,' Donated to Catholic Diocese of Grand Rapids." https://www.mlive.com/news/grand-rapids/2022/03/artprize-2011-winner-crucifixion-donated-to-catholic-diocese-of-grand-rapids.html.

9. *Hard Knocks*. 2021. Season 17. Aired 2021 on HBO.

10. Gaines, Cork. "Why Tom Brady Was Overlooked in the NFL Draft and Why It Was More Luck That Led Him to the Patriots." Business Insider. February 5, 2022. https://www.businessinsider.com/new-england-patriots-draft-tom-brady-sixth-round-pick-2022-2.

11. "Malala Yousafzai Biographical." From *The Nobel Prizes 2014*. Watson Publishing, 2015. NobelPrize.org. https://www.nobelprize.org/prizes/peace/2014/yousafzai/biographical/.

12. Scott, Ridley, dir. *Gladiator*. DreamWorks, 2000.

13. "Tiger Woods Completes Improbable Comeback, Wins 2019 Masters Championship." NBC Sports. April 14, 2019. https://www.nbcsports.com/bayarea/golf/tiger-woods-completes-improbable-comeback-wins-2019-masters-championship.

14. Krishnamurthy, Aaditya. "Michael Jordan's Secret to Success: 'I've Missed More Than 9000 Shots in My Career. I've Lost Almost 300 Games... I've Failed Over and Over and Over Again in My Life. And That Is Why I Succeed.'" Fadeaway World. January 26, 2022. https://fadeawayworld.net/nba-media/michael-jordans-secret-to-success-ive-missed-more-than-9000-shots-in-my-career-ive-lost-almost-300-games-ive-failed-over-and-over-and-over-again-in-my-life-and-that-is-why-i-succeed.

15. Evans, Tony. *Tony Evans' Book of Illustrations*. Moody, 2009, p. 324.